I'M TRYING TO
HELP
SOMEBODY

I'M TRYING TO HELP SOMEBODY

Daily Devotions John through Revelation

RODRICK A. SMITH

XULON ELITE

Xulon Press
2301 Lucien Way #415
Maitland, FL 32751
407.339.4217
www.xulonpress.com

Paperback ISBN-13: 978-1-66285-642-6
Ebook ISBN-13: 978-1-66285-643-3

DEDICATED TO

My three ladies,
Irma Jean (wife)
Angela Patrice (daughter)
Noa Gisele (granddaughter)

I would like to thank Ms. Rosa Holliday for her invaluable assistance in this endeavor.

Introduction

In March of 2020 the world was suddenly thrown into an unexpected and unforeseen crisis. The COVID-19 pandemic brought business as usual to a screeching halt. People were dying as others became ill but recovered. Many are presently coping with the long-term effects of this dreaded illness. Families were separated from one another, and multitudes died alone, with some saying their final goodbyes over Facetime and phone conversations.

Because of safety concerns, many houses of worship cancelled all services and activities. Because of our church closure and our need for daily spiritual nourishment, I felt compelled to write daily devotionals/readings for our congregation. They were posted daily on Facebook and our church website. These writings served as a source of encouragement for me, our congregation, and hopefully, for many others.

Sometimes while preaching, I have the habit of saying, "I'm trying to help somebody." With the offering of this book, that's what I'm attempting to do. It is my prayer that these daily writings will be a blessing to all who read and meditate on them. May God be glorified in and through them.

Foreword

Priest, pastor, and author Walter Russell Bowie has written in his book, *When the World Was Dark*, the church began long before there was such a thing as a special building where members might be accustomed to come together. When Jesus left the little town of Nazareth to tell people in all the land about God, He said to some men, "Come follow me." Once while in their fishing boats, Peter, Andrew, James, and John left their boats and nets and followed Jesus.

That is devotion, loyalty, enthusiasm. One by one, more were added until they became the Twelve. Other men and women also followed Jesus. The church needs and thrives on instruction, information, and inspiration that come from God.

Today, a large part of the church knows little about the scriptures. Many churches are in the courts or divided under the same roof because they are not governed by scripture and have not devoted themselves to Christ. Often the smallest meeting at church is the prayer meeting.

For members of the church, there should always be daily devotions. Pastor Rodrick Smith has meticulously dissected passages of the New Testament from the gospel of John to the book of Revelation. He has given us new insights on these chapters without losing the original message of the authors.

The true Christian/church member knows there is no substitute for prayer and the study of scriptures. True believers are praying and studying to rediscover the power and mission of the church. Pastor Smith aids us greatly in this devotional work.

Dr. C. E. McLain, Pastor
Little Union Baptist Church
Shreveport, Louisiana

In Him was life, and the life was the light of men. (John 1:4)

Jesus, the Word, is the source of life and light. At the creation, the Word of God called light into existence that there might be life in the world. Life is in the Word, not simply through Him. And as the life, the Word communicates light. The life that John speaks of is the blessed life; life that satisfies, being indwelt by God. It expresses all of the highest and best which Christ is, and which He gives to the saints. The life that He gives is the highest blessedness of the creature.

Our Lord and Savior Jesus Christ brought life and immortality to light in His gospel as the dispenser of moral and spiritual light. The light that shown through Him was the perfect knowledge and representation of God. If we've seen Him, we've seen the Father. "In Him was life, and the life was the light of men" (John 1:14). The light of men is the light which shines for men to give them the means of recognizing the giver of life. We thank and praise God for life and light.

The light shines in the darkness, and the darkness has not overcome it. (John 1:5)

The Voice Bible presents John 1:5 in this way, "A light that thrives in the depths of darkness, *blazes through murky bottoms. It cannot and will not be quenched.*" Darkness is no match for light. Even a small candle can dispel darkness from a room. The moral and spiritual darkness of this fallen world will never be able to extinguish the light of the Lord Jesus Christ. The life that was in Him was the light of men. Wherever light shows up, darkness has to flee; the two cannot co-exist.

At the beginning of the creation, the earth was without form and void, and darkness was over the face of the deep. And God said, "Let there be light," and there was light. This was the condition of our lives; spiritually empty, undeveloped, and dark. But when light showed up, things began to happen. The same God who made the world makes men. And, until men are able to see the light of the gospel of the glory of Christ, they will continue to stumble in darkness. But the good news is that the darkness will never overcome the light.

That attempt has been made throughout history. Satan and his demons have always tried to exterminate the life and extinguish the light. It was attempted when Israel was enslaved in Egypt. It was attempted when Herod commanded the slaughter of the innocents. It was attempted when Jesus was tested in the wilderness. But the light yet shines. Jesus said, "I am the light of the world. Anyone who follows Me will never walk in darkness but will have the light of life." (John 8:12)

The two disciples heard him say this, and they followed Jesus. (John 1:37)

John the Baptist was sent from God to bear witness about the Light, that all might believe through him. He was not that Light, but came to bear witness about that Light. John knew his place and understood the assignment given to him from God. John understood that even though he was Jesus's elder by a few months, and his ministry began before Jesus's ministry, He also understood that Jesus was the preexistent Word that became flesh. John knew his place and his purpose. As John announced the coming of the Lamb of God, he gained followers who stood with him and he with them. But when Jesus began His ministry, John's disciples became Jesus's disciples. Jesus said that John was the greatest among those born of women. And great men don't call disciples to themselves; they point men in the direction of the greatest Man.

John directed their attention to the Lamb of God, who takes away the sin of the world. John's followers heard him and followed Jesus. We must take care that the Lord's local churches don't become personality cults, focused on human personalities. We are to behold Jesus! We are to see, focus on, observe, listen to, and follow Him. No one will be saved by our names. Acts 4:12 says, "And there is salvation in no one else, for there is no other name under heaven given among men by which we must be saved." Follow Jesus!

The wind blows where it wishes, and you hear its sound, but you do not know where it comes from or where it goes. So it is with everyone who is born of the Spirit. (John 3:8)

None of us have actually seen the wind. But all of us have seen the effects of the wind. None of us can fully understand or control the wind. But all of us are capable of hearing it and harnessing its power. In the same way the Holy Spirit produces observable effects in the life of every born-again believer. There are mysteries in nature and in the life of the redeemed. The inner workings of the Holy Spirit in the life of the redeemed remain a mystery. At the beginning of the creation, the Spirit of God was hovering over the face of the waters. Then things began to happen. It's a mystery. Mary the mother of Jesus was found to be with child from the Holy Spirit and brought forth a Son. It's a mystery. In one Spirit, we were all baptized into one body and were all made to drink of one Spirit. It's a mystery. Every born-again believer experiences the indwelling presence of the Holy Spirit. It's all a mystery.

We are not aware of all God does or how He does it, but we are thankful for His doings. God has given us His Spirit that we might be empowered to live the Christian life. The Christian life cannot be lived by natural human strength and wisdom. God saves us and equips us to live the Spirit-filled life. No one can see the Holy Spirit within us, but they can see the evidence of His presence; the fruit that is produced in us by the Holy Spirit. The fruit of the Spirit is love, joy, peace, patience, kindness, goodness, faithfulness, gentleness, and self-control. I don't know how He does it. It's a mystery. But I'm glad He does.

Whoever believes in the Son has eternal life; whoever does not obey the Son shall not see life, but the wrath of God remains on him. (John 3:36)

The third chapter of John's Gospel begins with the necessity of the new birth. Unless one is born again, he cannot see the kingdom of God, nor can he enter the kingdom of God. Midway through the chapter, we are presented with what Max Lucado calls and is the title of his book, *3:16: The Numbers of Hope*. John 3:16 says, "For God so loved the world, that He gave His only Son, that whoever believes in Him should not perish but have eternal life." Whoever believes in the Son has eternal life. We are saved by grace through faith. Faith is basically belief and trust. But it is much more than giving mental assent to a given set of facts. James reminds us that the demons believe and tremble; but there is no salvation for them.

Saving faith is believing with the heart, which is the seat of the mind, emotions, and will. This means believing with the entire inner person. Genuine saving faith always leads to a life of active obedience. The person who practices a life of disobedience consistently and unashamedly shall not see the life or enter the kingdom Jesus promises. Belief and obedience go hand-in-hand. The verse says, "Whoever believes in the Son has eternal life." It says, "Whoever does not obey the Son shall not see life, but the wrath of God remains on him." The wrath of God is His necessary, just, and righteous retribution against sin. Prior to our salvation we were by nature children of wrath, but now we have been delivered from the wrath to come. For God has not destined us for wrath, but to obtain salvation through our Lord Jesus Christ.

And he himself believed, and all his household.
(John 4:53)

Just as the prophet stands before the people on behalf of God, the priest stands before God on behalf of the people. A principle taught in the Bible is that of the male head of a household serving as the family priest. As the spiritual leader of the family, he stands before God on behalf of his spouse and children. Just as God responded to the priestly intercession of those chosen for the office, He does the same for the family priest: the spiritual head of the household. Jesus was asked by a royal official to heal his son who is at the point of death. This unnamed man did not come to Jesus in an official government capacity; he came to him as a father desperately seeking healing for his dying son. It is implied in the original language that this father was repeatedly begging Jesus to come and heal his son.

This father paid no attention to Jesus's criticism of the Galilean sign-seekers, but said, "Sir, come down before my son dies." Jesus promised him that his son would live, and at the same hour his fever left him. The father knew that this was Jesus's doing. And he himself believed, along with all his household. There may have been a mother in the household who was worried about her son. Perhaps there were siblings in the household who were concerned about their brother. There was the dying son who was certainly fearful of losing his own life. But the father had heard about Jesus and set out to stand before Him on behalf of his son. Jesus not only physically healed the son, He spiritually healed the household. When the father believed, the likelihood of the household being saved increased exponentially. Even though this is not a guarantee, it is a general truth. Everything begins in the home.

This, the first of His signs, Jesus did at Cana in Galilee, and manifested His glory. This was now the second sign that Jesus did. (John 2:11; 4:54)

The apostle John uses the term *signs* in reference to Jesus's miracles. These were signs with significance. They pointed toward something beyond the sign itself. The signs were signals and tokens with a spiritual end and purpose. They were miracles, which led to something out of and beyond themselves. We often see signs on the roadside when traveling. The signs are not the destination but offer guidance in getting there. God never does anything just because He can.

Everything He does has a purpose. Jesus did not perform miracles just to put His power on display; He was not a showoff, and He never shows out.

Jesus's miracles were always miracles of mercy, which attended to a specific need, manifested His glory, and awakened or confirmed His disciples' faith in Him. There were also instances where He performed miracles after a pronouncement of faith was made by its beneficiary. The signs that Jesus performed revealed various aspects of His person and work. They all had eternal significance for those who had eyes to see.

*Whoever does not honor the Son does not honor
the Father who sent Him. (John 5:23)*

The most important decision a person ever makes in life
is choosing to accept or reject Jesus Christ as Lord and Savior.
This decision has eternal consequences because Jesus Christ
has been appointed judge of all mankind. If the Father has
appointed the Son as judge, wisdom dictates that we honor the
Father by honoring the Son whom He has appointed. To dishonor the Son is to dishonor the Father. Even earthly judges are
given respect, and we address them in court as "Your Honor."
To fail to render proper respect to the earthly judge will cause
one to be held in contempt. The writer of the epistle to the
Hebrews says, "And just as it is appointed for man to die once,
and after that comes judgment" (Heb. 9:27). This judgment
will be rendered by Jesus Christ, and His decision will be final.

But God the Father has also appointed Him as the Savior
of mankind. It is far better to know Him as Savior rather than
facing Him as Judge. God has provided the Savior that we so
desperately need. Jesus said, "Truly, truly, I say to you, whoever
hears My word and believes Him who sent Me has eternal life.
He does not come into judgment, but has passed from death
to life." (John 5:24) Jesus also said, "I am the way, and the
truth, and the life. No one comes to the Father except through
Me." (John 14:6) Honor the Father by honoring the Son whom
He has sent.

For on Him God the Father has set His seal.
(John 6:27)

The seal is a mark of authenticity, authority, ownership, and security. Our Lord's power to do His Father's will by giving eternal life to all who believed, rested in the authority vested in Him by the Father. Jesus was authenticated and endorsed by the Father at His baptism by John the Baptist in the Jordan River. At this event, He was sealed by the voice of the Father and by the bestowal of the Spirit, setting Him apart to do His Father's will. What God did for His Son, He does for all of His children. Paul says to the saints at Ephesus, "In Him you also, when you heard the word of truth, the gospel of your salvation, and believed in Him, were sealed with the promised Holy Spirit." (Eph. 1:13) At the very moment we believed, we were sealed with the Holy Spirit who had been promised to us. When we were sealed, we became God's special possession and began to experience the safety and security of His everlasting arms.

The sealing of the Holy Spirit guarantees our eternal salvation. Because God has sealed us, we are the authentic children of God. His Spirit bears witness with our spirit that we are children of God. Because God has sealed us, He has authority over our lives. This authority was given to the Son after His resurrection; He is King of kings and Lord of lords. Because God has sealed us, He owns us by creation and redemption. We are not our own; we were bought with a price. Because God has sealed us, we are eternally secure. Jesus said, "All that the Father gives Me will come to Me, and whoever comes to Me I will never cast out." (John 6:37)

I will raise him up on the last day. (see John 6:39–40, 44, 54)

The glorious hope of every born-again believer is to be resurrected and glorified together with Christ at the last day. At that time, we will be like Him and see Him as He is, in our glorified state. In Jesus's "bread of life" discourse, He places a strong emphasis on the resurrection at the last day. He proclaims four times, "I will raise him up on the last day." It is the will of God that Christ should lose none of those given Him by the Father; but He will raise him up on the last day. Everyone who looks on the Son and believes in Him will have eternal life; and He will raise him up on the last day. No one can come to Christ unless they are drawn by the Father. Those who are drawn by the Father are given to the Son, and He will raise them up on the last day.

Jesus often spoke of spiritual realities by using physical terminology. He said, "Unless you eat the flesh of the Son of Man and drink His blood, you have no life in you. Whoever feeds on My flesh and drinks My blood has eternal life." (John 6:53-54) Jesus was not promoting cannibalism or the consumption of blood. But He was speaking of the spiritual hunger and thirst that can be satisfied only by believing and trusting in Him; namely His person, and His death, burial, and resurrection. Everyone who believes with the heart will confess with the mouth that Jesus is Lord; and He will raise him up on the last day.

Now Jesus loved Martha and her sister and Lazarus. (John 11:5)

When Lazarus became ill, his sisters knew that Jesus would be concerned because of His love for them. The sisters sent for Jesus because God's ears are always attentively open to our cries. But Jesus didn't respond right away. We expect love to act immediately, but God's delays are not His denials. Divine delays often bring even greater blessings. Even though it was dangerous for Jesus to return to Judea, love takes courage, and perfect love casts out fear. Love has a way of comforting us. Jesus said, "Your brother will rise again." These are comforting words. Love doesn't pour salt on wounds. As a result, Martha moved from, "Lord, if You had been here," to "Lord, I believe." Jesus identifies with our sorrows. Jesus wept. Knowing what He would do, He still wept with them. We ought to feel the pain of others. To sympathize is to share in a feeling with someone. This should lead us to serving others and not ourselves. Serve somebody as they travel through the valleys of life. A heart filled with love will find a way to lift somebody's burden. For Lazarus, the stone was taken away, he came out of the tomb, and he was unbound and set free.

How did God demonstrate His own love toward us? According to Romans 5:8, "God shows His love for us in that while we were still sinners, Christ died for us." God's love for us becomes up close and personal. It becomes specific, as determined by our unique situations.

And there was much muttering about Him among the people. While some said, "He is a good man," others said, "No, He is leading the people astray." Some of them wanted to arrest Him, but no one laid hands on Him. (John 7:12, 44)

As Jesus moved among the people during the time of His earthly ministry, there were many opinions of Him. He was accused of being demon possessed. He was considered to be one who had no regard for the Law of Moses. He was also accused of being a blasphemer. Some believed that nothing good could come from Nazareth; therefore, He could not possibly be the Messiah. Many did not believe in Him but followed for the benefit of the miracles. There was much "muttering" about Him among the people. Some people believed He was a good man. He saved the wedding feast by turning water into wine. He fed the five thousand with the lad's lunch. He healed the government official's son and the man who had been paralyzed for thirty-eight years. All He ever did was good.

But there were others who said, "No, He is leading the people astray." These individuals did not argue about His good deeds, but instead, accused Him of being a deceiver. Members of the religious establishment wanted Him arrested. But this would happen only according to God's plan and purpose. People have many opinions of us. Even the good that we do is sometimes questioned and looked upon with suspicion. There are those who would rid themselves of us if they could. But like Jesus, our times are in God's hands, and we need not fear the hands of man.

"Jesus said to them, 'If God were your Father, you would love Me, for I came from God and I am here" (John 8:42).

Jesus is speaking to the scribes and Pharisees on the subject of divine Fatherhood. The word *father* is mentioned some twenty-one times in this chapter. The universal fatherhood of God is a contradiction of the teachings of Jesus. First John 5:1 says "Everyone who believes that Jesus is the Christ has been born of God." We are made the children of God by faith and born into His family. There are certain characteristics we would possess if God were our Father. If God were our Father, we would love His Son. God is love, and His children are lovers. We would begin by loving His Son because God sent Him. We would love what God sends because we know that every good gift and every perfect gift is from above.

We would also receive the words of His Son. Jesus said, "I am the truth." God the Father said, "This is My beloved Son, with whom I am well pleased; listen to Him." (Matt. 17:5) God's children will hear His Word. The sheep know the voice of their Shepherd and follow Him. We would also have a desire to do His will. In a general sense, children have the desires of their father. Jesus came to do the will of His Father who sent Him.

The old saying goes, "The apple doesn't fall far from the tree." Self-examination is always in order. Do I love Jesus, the Son of God? Do I receive (believe and internalize) His words? Do I have a desire to do God's will? In the words of Dr. C. E. McLain, "Grade your own paper."

We must work the works of Him who sent Me while it is day; night is coming, when no one can work. (John 9:4)

Jesus was the perfect example of redeeming the time. In the gospels He repeatedly stated that He was sent by the Father. During His earthly ministry among men, He only did what His Father sent Him to do; and He only spoke what His Father sent Him to speak. There were no wasted moments in His life. At the age of twelve, He proclaimed to His mother and earthly father, "I must be about My Father's business." Dr. Luke speaks of how He subjected Himself in constant obedience to them. As a result, He grew in wisdom and in stature and in favor with God and man. The next eighteen years of His life were lived in obscurity. When He ascends from the baptismal waters at the age of thirty, the Father endorses Him by declaring, "This is My beloved Son, in whom I am well pleased." From birth to the age of twelve, God was pleased. From the age of twelve to the beginning of His ministry at the age of thirty, God the Father was pleased.

From the beginning of His ministry to its climax at Golgotha and His subsequent burial and resurrection, the Father was pleased. God the Father was pleased with His Son's entire earthly existence. Jesus worked among men while He was alive, knowing that He had an appointment with death. But He did say, "We must work." As disciples of Christ we must follow His example of "redeeming the time." We must work the works that have been assigned to us while we are living because the night is coming, and our opportunities to work will cease. Why do you stand here idle all day?

And many came to Him. And they said, "John did no sign, but everything that John said about this man was true." And many believed in Him there. (John 10:41–42)

Jesus constantly spoke of His oneness with the Father. And even after witnessing His wonderful works, many of the Jews held fast to their unbelief. Jesus explained that the reason for their unbelief was because they were not a part of His flock. He said, "My sheep hear My voice, and I know them, and they follow Me. I and the Father are one." These Jews picked up stones to stone Him. A few minutes later they sought to arrest Him, but He escaped from their hands. They had a problem with who they perceived to be a man, making Himself God. To them, this was blasphemy. Jesus went away to the place where John had been baptizing. But there were others who came to Him who eventually believed. They said, "John did no sign (miracle), but everything that John said about this man was true." By this time, John the Baptist was dead. But as these Jews find themselves with Jesus in the place where John baptized, they recalled to mind his words concerning Jesus.

There may be nothing sensational about your personality or your ministry. You may labor in the background as others take center stage. You may serve in the shadows while others stand in the spotlight. But be sure to speak the truth about the Lord Jesus Christ. Point people in the direction of the Savior. Be a witness for Him. Like John the Baptist, we must decrease as the Lord increases. Even without a sign (miracle), some will believe.

So Thomas, called the Twin, said to his fellow disciples, "Let us also go, that we may die with Him." (John 11:16)

The apostle Thomas, who was also called Didymus, is known in church history as "Doubting Thomas." Both names actually mean "twin." Thomas is probably best known for his inability to believe that Jesus had indeed risen from the dead. Thomas was not present when Jesus first appeared to His disciples after the resurrection. Upon hearing of the appearance, Thomas said, "Unless I see in His hands the mark of the nails, and place my finger into the mark of the nails, and place my hand into His side, I will never believe." (John 20:25) Eight days later, Jesus appeared again to the disciples, including Thomas. After Thomas was invited by Jesus to touch the nail prints and put his hand into His side, his response was, "My Lord and my God!" But there was more to Thomas than his propensity to doubt.

Many of the Jews, especially those of the religious establishment, had grown hostile toward Jesus and sought to arrest Him on more than one occasion, and stone Him on a few others. Being fully aware of this hostility toward Him, Jesus decided to return to Bethany to raise Lazarus from the dead. Being full of courage, Thomas said, "Let us also go." Being full of pessimism, He said, "that we may die with Him." Thomas spoke words of loyal devotion, courage, and pessimism. Even though he has a negative outlook, he appears to be willing to die with Christ. Thomas takes the lead, and they all go to Bethany. Don't be too hard on him or others.

Because on account of him many of the Jews were going away and believing in Jesus. (John 12:11)

After the raising of Lazarus from the dead, large crowds were curious about Jesus the wonder worker and Lazarus the walking witness. Lazarus who had been dead became a living witness. We too have been raised to newness of life, and out of curiosity, people want to see us. Because Lazarus was a living, walking witness, after his resurrection, he had enemies. Every born-again believer will be attacked by the enemy. The enemy wants to silence your testimony and weaken your witness. He also seeks to steal, kill, and destroy.

Because of the transforming power of his witness, the enemy wanted to kill Lazarus and put him back into the tomb out of which Jesus had delivered him. He also wants to put us back into the grave and the grave clothes out of which Jesus has delivered us. But because of the new life seen in Lazarus, many believed in Jesus and were converted. The Bible doesn't record a single word ever spoken by Lazarus, but because of him, people are coming to faith in Jesus. Who are we influencing as a result of new life in Christ? Who have we led to Christ? A living witness can make a difference in this world. A living witness has influence.

So the Pharisees said to one another, "You see that you are gaining nothing. Look, the world has gone after Him." (John 12:19)

After Lazarus was raised from the dead many of the Jews believed in Jesus. But some of them reported this sign to His enemies, namely the chief priests and Pharisees. Soon afterward, they called together members of the Sanhedrin Counsel to discuss what action they should take. At this point they begin to plot the death of Jesus. But what they did not know was that Jesus's death and resurrection would bring together Jews and Gentiles who would make up the church. At that point, Judas was about to betray Jesus for thirty pieces of silver. He was a greedy man who served as treasurer of the group, and often helped himself to what was in the treasury. The next day was the Lord's triumphal entry into Jerusalem. The crowds anticipated Him and hailed Him as Deliverer, Messiah, and King of Israel. As a result, His enemies became even more hateful and jealous. Hatred and jealousy are dangerous emotions, especially for those who harbor them. The Lord's enemies were right; they were gaining nothing but losing their very souls.

Generally speaking, people were following Jesus, which meant they were no longer following His enemies. As in the case with Jesus, God will sometimes allow your enemies to get to you. But they will gain nothing from it but a temporary sense of accomplishment. There is always a bigger picture being painted that we are not aware of. We are but one small piece of God's divinely designed puzzle. Eventually, even those under the earth (in hell) will bow the knee and confess that Jesus Christ is Lord, to the glory of God the Father. But this will be submission too late.

If you know these things, blessed are you if you do them. (John 13:17)

For many years, I have heard many people say, "When you know better, you should do better." This saying has always made sense to me. After all, wisdom is the proper application of knowledge. The purpose of possessing knowledge is to gain wisdom through its application. Jesus presented to His disciples an illustration of humility and servanthood. He was their Teacher and Lord but fleshed out an example of serving others in the lowliest manner. Sometimes we must come down in order to lift others for their good and God's glory. Nothing should be beneath us when it comes to serving one another. The truth of the matter is, a servant is not greater than his Master, and a messenger is not greater than the One who sent him. Jesus is our Master and Lord.

Mary stooped to wash the Master's feet, and the Lord stooped to wash the disciples' feet (and Judas's also). The people of God are most blessed in knowing and doing the will of God. This is really the secret to living a life of spiritual abundance: knowing and doing the will of God. Therefore, my dear brothers and sisters, be steadfast, immovable, always excelling in the Lord's work, because you know that your labor in the Lord is not in vain (1 Cor. 15:58). Knowing and doing leads to a wonderful state of blessedness.

Truly, truly, I say to you, whoever believes in Me will also do the works that I do; and greater works than these will he do, because I am going to the Father. (John 14:12)

According to the book of Acts, the believers were first called Christians at Antioch of Syria. This was a term of derision that identified them as those who belong to Christ. Eventually, however, Christians used it of themselves as a name of honor, not of shame. Jesus said, "Whoever believes in Me (Christians) will also do the works that I do." Jesus said, "I am the light of the world." He also said to His disciples, "You are the light of the world." Jesus washed His disciples' feet and commanded them to wash one another's feet. Jesus was a Man of prayer and taught them to pray. Jesus healed the sick and cast out demons. He empowered His apostles to do the same. They did the same works that Jesus did. Even though Jesus did many wonderful works that we will never do, He still commissions us to emulate Him by doing what He did and by living the way He lived.

Jesus also said, "And greater works than these will he do." Jesus did not mean that the works we would do would be greater in power. He meant that they would be greater in extent and scope. The ministry of Jesus was confined to the area of Palestine. But according to the Great Commission, His disciples would be empowered by the Holy Spirit to be His witnesses to the end of the earth. They would make disciples of all nations, baptizing and teaching even to the end of the age. Jesus's earthly ministry was limited in time and space but not in power. After over two thousand years of church history, Christians have carried the gospel message to billions of people all over the world. That's greater in scope and extent. And we press on.

*Peace I leave with you; My peace I give to you.
Not as the world gives do I give to you. Let not
your hearts be troubled, neither let them be
afraid. (John 14:27)*

It is the will of God that none of His children go through life troubled and afraid. He wants all of us to enjoy the peace that He provides. John, chapter fourteen, begins with "Let not your hearts be troubled." There are many reasons for believers to not be troubled (disturbed with various emotions) or afraid (fearful and timid). As Jesus prepared the disciples for His departure, He made some very comforting promises to them (and us). He promised to leave His peace with them. This is that tranquil state of the soul assured of its salvation through Christ, and subsequently content with its earthly situation, whatever it may be. He promised to prepare a place for them in His Father's house, and while He's away, they wouldn't be left as orphans. He promised to send to them another Helper of the same kind—the Holy Spirit. Jesus was (and is) the truth, and He would send to them the Spirit of truth who would teach them all things and bring to their remembrance all that He had said to them. He assured them that He was in the Father, and that they were in Him, and that He was in them. He who loves Jesus will be loved by the Father, and Jesus will love him and manifest Himself to them. Anyone who loves Jesus will keep His Word, and His Father will love him, and the Father and Son will come to him and make their home with him. Because He has given us His peace, along with so many promises, we have no reason to be troubled or afraid.

If the world hates you, know that it has hated
Me before it hated you. (John 15:18)

Jesus never led His disciples to believe that if they followed Him, their lives would become easier, and everyone would love them and treat them well. He was always forthcoming about the conditions and cost of discipleship. Jesus did not come into the world to be friends with the devil, and neither should His followers. This is one of the problems with the modern-day church. The church seeks to be like the world, and the world has no interest in being like the church. As a matter of fact, the world is not interested in anything the church has to offer unless it appeals to the flesh. I need to state this truth very plainly. The world hates the church and every born-again believer who is a part of it. The apostle John's writings are rich in references to the relation of believers to the world, considered as a fallen universe hostile to God. Jesus Himself referred to Satan as the ruler of this world. He is the leader of this evil world system in its rebellion against God. This evil world system hates Jesus and those who follow Him. Jesus said, "A servant is not greater than his master. If they persecuted Me, they will also persecute you." This evil world system hates God the Father and God the Son. Therefore, we shouldn't be surprised by its hatred of us. Jesus said, "I have said these things to you, that in Me you may have peace. In the world you will have tribulation. But take heart; I have overcome the world." (John 16:33)

Oh righteous Father, even though the world does not know You, I know You, and these know that You have sent Me. (John 17:25)

In the Lord's "High Priestly Prayer," He used the word *world* some eighteen times. In John's vocabulary, the world is set against God. John is referring to the evil world system that is ruled by Satan, and stands in opposition to all of the plans and purposes of God. As Jesus prayed for Himself, He asked that His Father would glorify Him with the glory He possessed before the world existed. He proclaimed that He had manifested His Father's name to the people He gave Him out of the world. As He began to pray for His disciples, He declared that He was not praying for the world, but for those whom His Father had given Him. Jesus was now at the end of His earthly ministry and would leave His disciples in the world. They had received His word, and the world had hated them because they were not of the world, just as He was not of the world. He didn't pray that they would be taken out of the world, but that they be protected from the evil one.

As He was sent into the world, now He sent them into the world. At that point, the Lord looked into the future and included all believers in this prayer. He prayed that we might be one, so that the world might believe that the Father sent the Son. He prayed that we might be where He is, to see the glory He had before the foundation of the world. Even though Jesus did not pray for the world, He did pray for His followers so that they would function as witnesses to the world, "that the world may believe that You have sent Me." We are in the world, but not of the world, to bear witness to the world.

They cried out again, "Not this man, but Barabbas!" Now Barabbas was a robber. (John 18:40)

Every day we have to make situational decisions that require us to choose between Jesus and something or someone else. In order that he might wash his hands of deciding Jesus's fate, Pilate gave the Jerusalem mob the responsibility of choosing between Jesus and Barabbas as one to be set free. The crowd chose Barabbas and demanded that Jesus be crucified. Barabbas means "son of the father." We don't know anything about his father, but the record says some things about Barabbas. The apostle John describes him as a robber (one who unlawfully seizes plunder). He took what He wanted. Matthew depicts him as a notorious (widely and unfavorably known) prisoner. He was experienced in gangsterism. Mark and Luke report him as being among rebels in prison, who had committed murder and insurrection. Life, law, and order meant nothing to him.

On the other hand, there is Jesus. He is the Son of His Father, who is God almighty. His name means "Savior." He is Immanuel, or "God with us." He is the Christ (Messiah or Anointed One). He worked miracles of mercy and spoke only the truth. But this is who the Jerusalem mob rejected. They shouted, "Away with this man, and release to us Barabbas!" They boldly cried, "Let Him be crucified, and His blood be on us and our children." Consider here the love of God. In our former lives, we have boldly made foolish declarations and bad choices concerning Jesus. But motivated by love, grace, and mercy, He chose us before the foundation of the world. And as a result of faith in Him, we and our believing children are covered by His blood. Always choose Jesus!

Jesus answered him, "You would have no authority over me at all unless it had been given you from above." (John 19:11)

Under the sovereign hand of God, Pontius Pilate was Roman governor of Judea from AD 26 to 36 and had his part to play in the interrogation, sentencing, and crucifixion of Jesus. He is the one man of all Roman officials who is named in the Apostles' Creed. The Apostles' Creed reads concerning Jesus, "He suffered under Pontius Pilate." When Jesus was being interrogated by Pilate, He was asked, "Where are you from?" Jesus refused to answer him. Pilate responded by saying, "You will not speak to me? Do you not know that I have authority to release you and authority to crucify you?" Jesus's answer to Pilate reassures us of the sovereignty of God. He exercises complete control over His entire creation. Nothing happens unless God directly does it or permissively allows it to happen. Even the worst evil that befalls us is under the authority of our sovereign God. All of our trials, tribulations, suffering, and pain are part of His divine plan.

Isaiah says concerning Christ, "Yet it was the will of the LORD to crush him; He has put him to grief; when his soul makes an offering for sin." (Isa. 53:10) Pilate's authority did not come from the Roman Emperor. It came from an almighty and sovereign God. Even though men and women are free moral agents, exercising freedom of speech and actions, they all enter and exit this world under the sovereignty of God. Believers can go through life, knowing that God is the ultimate authority in this world. Now, ain't that good news!

On the evening of that day, the first day of the week, the doors being locked where the disciples were for fear of the Jews, Jesus came and stood among them and said to them, "Peace be with you." (John 20:19)

Jesus never mentioned His death without also mentioning His resurrection. He possessed power to lay down His life and power to take it up again. To be sure, His words were prophetic, but they also served as a means of assuring His disciples that death was not the end. On the day of the Lord's resurrection, He appeared to the disciples while they are gathered in a locked room for fear of the Jews. They had had a week that they would never forget. It began with the Lord's triumphal entry into Jerusalem, with the people shouting, "Hosanna! Blessed is He who comes in the name of the LORD! The King of Israel!" But the week ended with the people shouting, "Give us Barabbas and crucify Jesus!" Barabbas was set free, and Jesus was crucified and buried. But just as He predicted, on the third day He arose.

On this resurrection day evening, the disciples were locked in a room because of their fear of the Jews. They were afraid that Jesus's fate would become their own. But He came and stood among them, and they were glad. His presence has a way of bringing peace to the weary and fearful soul. He was dead but is now alive. He greeted them with peace and granted peace to them. Without His presence, there was fear. In His presence, there was peace. Jesus breathed on them and said, "Receive the Holy Spirit." Because of the abiding presence of the Holy Spirit, every believer experiences peace with God and the peace of God. Fear not; the fruit of the Spirit is peace.

Simon Peter said to them, "I am going fishing."
They said to him, "We will go with you." They
went out and got into the boat, but that night
they caught nothing. (John 21:3)

When Jesus called His first disciples, they were working at their profession as fishermen. On that occasion, Jesus was standing by the Sea of Galilee. Jesus used Peter's boat as a platform from which to teach the people. This happened after a long night of toilsome fishing and catching nothing. Jesus commanded Peter to put the boat out into the deep and let down his nets for a catch; Peter obeyed. The catch was so large, they filled two boats that began to sink. Jesus said to Peter, "From now on, you will be catching men." At that very moment, they left everything and followed Jesus. According to the gospel accounts, they didn't fish again until the night before the Lord's third post-resurrection appearance. And just like the night before, they were called to catch men, after having fished all night and having caught nothing. Again, Jesus was standing by the Sea of Galilee. He gave instructions to these seasoned fishermen, and they hauled in another large catch. On the land, Jesus had a fire in place, with fish laid out on it, and bread. He told them to bring some of the fish that they had just caught. He then told them to come and have breakfast. None of the disciples asked Him who He was. They knew it was the Lord. Jesus took the bread and gave it to them, and so with the fish. When the miraculous happens in our lives, we know it is Jesus.

Sometimes present experiences are almost identical to past experiences, and the Lord stands in the midst of both, demonstrating His awesome power. We may go back and forth, but Jesus Christ is the same yesterday and today and forever.

He said to them, "It is not for you to know times or seasons that the Father has fixed by His own authority." (Acts 1:7)

Seasons are the main periods of the year in which each have their own distinctive weather. They are examples of God's perfect order in the world and represent the balanced cycle of creation and human life, which are sustained by God. Seasons are appointed, created, and sustained by God. There are also seasons of life. These are appropriate and appointed periods of time, which are part of the variety and development of human life and experience, and which influence human affairs. The times and seasons for individuals and nations are set by God, who works all things together toward the final fulfillment of His purposes. The seasons of life are not self-appointed. If it is not for us to know the times and seasons that the Father has fixed by His own authority, then certainly it is not for us to appoint the times and seasons of our lives. We live in a time when people who profess to be Christians believe they can control the seasons of life or live perpetually in only one season by the words they speak. It is now popular to hear people say, "I declare," or "I decree." Many professing Christians often declare it to be a certain "season" in their lives. This is error and possibly heresy! Heresy is a position or doctrine at variance with established, orthodox church doctrine. When the Scripture makes plain sense, it makes no sense to seek any other sense, lest we come to nonsense. I'm trying to help somebody.

*Every day the Lord added to their number those
who were being saved. (Acts 2:47)*

Psalm 127:1 says, "Unless the LORD builds the house, those who build it labor in vain." Jesus said, "I will build My church." To attempt to build or grow the Lord's church by way of human ingenuity is a vain and useless endeavor. This misguided exercise in spiritual futility causes one to be in competition with Christ Himself. It is also an attempt to usurp the authority that belongs exclusively to Christ, the Owner and Builder of the church. The church is the "called out" assembly of the saints. We are "called" to salvation; and inherent in the call to salvation is the call to a particular area of ministry. Every born-again believer was chosen in Christ before the foundation of the world, and predestined for adoption through Jesus Christ, according to the purpose of God's will. Jesus said to His disciples, "You did not choose Me, but I chose you that you should go and bear fruit and that your fruit should abide." (John 15:16) The church can grow numerically only when the Lord adds to it. We can use gimmicks and bow down to every religious fad and trend, but only the Lord can add to the church. Some may attempt to be the cool church, the hip church, or the happening church, and as a result attract the desired crowd. But only God can grow His church; and He grows it by adding saved souls. Let's be the church of the living God, the pillar and ground of the truth; and He will add those who are being saved.

*And he fixed his attention on them, expecting to
receive something from them. (Acts 3:5)*

Peter and John were going *up* to the temple with the
intention of looking *up* to God in prayer. Even when we pray
with bowed heads and closed eyes, our hearts are taking the
upward look. In their *upward* physical and spiritual mobility,
they encounter a man who's been down his entire life. He didn't
know anything about the *upward* life except for what he had
observed with his eyes and heard with his ears. He was carried
and laid at the Beautiful Gate daily. He depended on the hands
and hearts of others to sustain him. Every day, he was lifted
only to be let down. His life was an unending cycle of sameness. He saw Peter and John on their way into the temple, and
before he can ask for a handout, Peter extended to him a hand
up. Peter says to him, "Look at us." He was invited to take an
upward look as Peter and John look down *at* him, but not *on*
him. Peter and John didn't have what he wanted, but they do
have what he needed. Peter commanded him to *rise up* and
walk in the name of Jesus. Peter not only told him to *rise up*
and walk, but he extended a hand of fellowship and helped
him *rise up*. This man leaped *up*, stood *up*, and walked *up* into
the temple. This was the end of his lameness and sameness. He
looked *up*, rose *up*, stood *up*, leaped *up*, walked *up*, and sent
some praises *up*. Oh that men would praise the Lord for His
goodness, and for His wonderful works to the children of men
(Ps. 107:8).

Now when they saw the boldness of Peter and John, and perceived that they were uneducated, common men, they were astonished. And they recognized that they had been with Jesus. (Acts 4:13)

The resurrection of Jesus Christ was the turning point in the lives of the apostles, simply because they knew He was alive. After His resurrection He commanded them to wait for the promised Holy Spirit before engaging in any kind of ministry. After the infilling of the Holy Spirit, they were empowered to courageously stand and to fearlessly proclaim the truth about the death, burial, and resurrection of Jesus. The religious authorities witnessed the boldness of Peter and John, and were utterly amazed. The confidence of Peter and John was on full display. They said what needed to be said without any fear of consequences. They spoke openly and frankly, and were to the point. Even though it was known that they had no formal theological training, the religious leaders knew that they had been with Jesus. They had left all and followed Him. Peter and John had been with Jesus for over three years. They were members of the Lord's inner circle along with James, John's brother. They witnessed His miraculous works and were instructed by His teaching. Jesus taught them to pray, and His word was in them. They were saved, sanctified, and filled with the Holy Spirit. Can anyone recognize that we've been with Jesus?

Then they left the presence of the council,
rejoicing that they were counted worthy to
suffer dishonor for the name. (Acts 5:41)

Christian believers are empowered to be the Lord's witnesses, and witnessing will lead to suffering. We suffer because He suffered. Jesus was our suffering Savior. When we consider the suffering of the Lord's apostles, it always followed the working of signs and wonders, the saving of souls, the healing of the sick, and the preaching of His Word. On many occasions, their arrest and persecution was preceded by the jealousy of the Lord's enemies who had now become their enemies. Jesus did not come into the world to be friends with the devil, and neither should we. Friendship with the world is hostility toward God. The apostles had a strange and unusual response to their suffering. After having been arrested and imprisoned, they were miraculously freed by an angel of the Lord. The next morning, they were detained again by the authorities and reminded of the former command they were given to not preach in Jesus's name. The apostles then said, "We ought to obey God rather than men." They were then beaten and threatened, and commanded again to not speak in the name of Jesus. They left rejoicing that they were counted worthy to be treated shamefully on behalf of His name. What a strange and unusual response to suffering. How do we respond to Christian suffering? If we suffer with Him, we will reign with Him.

And they chose Stephen. (Acts 6:5)

Stephen was one of the seven men who were chosen to attend to the daily distribution of necessities in the early church. It would not have been good for the congregation had the apostles left the preaching of the Word to personally attend to this matter. Therefore, they appointed qualified men who were chosen by the multitude to perform this necessary function. All seven men had good reputations and were full of the Holy Spirit and wisdom. These qualities are a must for all who would serve as leaders in the Lord's church. But Stephen was a cut above the rest. He is the first to be mentioned by Luke and the first to be attacked by the enemies of the church. Why is this? Stephen was full of grace and power, which means he was controlled by and under the influence of both. God worked miracles through him. When the enemies of the church rose up to dispute with him, they could not withstand the wisdom and Spirit with which he spoke. He had the God-given ability to refute all of their false claims and accusations, and the Holy Spirit empowered him to stand and speak. Even after he was seized and brought before the Sanhedrin Council, his enemies saw that he had the appearance of one who had been in the presence of God. When the wisdom and Spirit of God indwells a person, even their enemies notice a calm, composed, and unflappable demeanor. A man's wisdom makes his face shine, and the hardness of his face is changed (Eccles. 8:1). Be cool, be calm, and be collected.

He said, "Look, I see the heavens opened and the Son of Man standing at the right hand of God!" (Acts 7:56)

There are many Scripture references in the Bible that speak of Jesus sitting at the right hand of God the Father. To be seated at the right hand of royalty is a high honor. But to be seated at "the right hand" of God is incomparably higher. To be seated at the right hand of God is to occupy the place of supreme privilege and power. When Stephen, the first Christian martyr was stoned to death, he gazed into heaven, saw the glory of God, and Jesus standing at His right hand. I've always wondered why Jesus was standing at the right hand of God rather than sitting, as He is usually depicted. There are times when we sit, watch, and listen as certain events take place. But I know from experience that some things touch us emotionally and move us to stand, give special attention, and respond. Our suffering Savior does not take our suffering lightly, especially when we are suffering for His name's sake. When we go through times of intense suffering and persecution, He doesn't just sit there. He is often moved to stand to His feet. Jesus knows all about our struggles, and He ever lives to intercede on our behalf; sometimes sitting and sometimes standing, but always sympathizing. That's good news!

This is a desert place. (Acts 8:26)

Philip was one of the seven men chosen to facilitate the daily distribution of food and finances in the sixth chapter of Acts. He became an effective preacher and missionary in the city of Samaria. Multitudes were saved as a result of his preaching and were witnesses of the miracles which God performed through him. Demons were exorcised, and many with physical deformities were healed. As a result, there was great joy in that city. While serving in this growing and flourishing ministry in Samaria, an angelic messenger from the Lord instructed Philip to leave Samaria and travel south of Jerusalem to a deserted place. Without question or hesitation he obeyed. Most people would have a problem with leaving multitudes to go to a deserted place. Many ministers are concerned about numbers and crowds, and wouldn't see this as a promotion or a directive from God. If Philip had sought counsel from colleagues in the ministry, he probably would have been discouraged from going to a deserted place. But the intimacy of Philip's relationship with God enabled him to discern the will of God for his ministry. And God's will for him was the only thing that mattered. Philip left the multitudes in Samaria and traveled the road that goes down from Jerusalem to Gaza. In that deserted place, the Holy Spirit directed him to an Ethiopian court official.

Philip explained the gospel to him and baptized him. The Ethiopian went on his way rejoicing, and the Holy Spirit carried Philip away to his next assignment. We are called to do God's bidding. We serve Him without personal ambitions and agendas, while moving at His command. Trust and obey!

> *"Saul, Saul, Why are you persecuting Me? I am Jesus, whom you are persecuting. But rise and enter the city, and you will be told what you are to do." (Acts 9:4-5)*

We are introduced to Saul of Tarsus in chapter seven during the infamous stoning of Stephen. He doesn't participate in the stoning but consented to Stephen's death and held the coats of the ones who murdered him. When confronted and called by Christ on the Damascus road, Saul was asked by the risen Christ, "Why are you persecuting Me?" He responded by asking, "Who are you, Lord?" The Lord then said, "I am Jesus, whom you are persecuting." Christ is the head of the church. All believers make up the church, which is the body of Christ. An attack on the body is an attack on the head. An attack on a member of the body of Christ is an attack on the head. Jesus introduced Himself to Saul, revealed to him the object of his attacks, and simultaneously enlisted him in the ministry. We talk about grace and mercy, and being used by God in spite of ourselves and our past. See with fresh eyes how God dealt with Saul. See with fresh eyes how God deals with us. He sometimes blinds us by the light of His countenance, knocks us down, opens our ears and hearts, and shows us Himself. He then commands us to get up, tells us where to go, and to wait for further instructions. When this happens, our lives are never the same. God has a reputation for stopping sinners in their tracks and changing the direction of their lives.

And he stayed in Joppa for many days with one
Simon, a tanner. (Acts 9:43)

There are three distinct groups of people in the New Testament who identify in some way with the Jews' religion. There are the Jews themselves, who practiced Judaism. There are the proselytes who were Gentiles who had converted to Judaism. And there were the God-fearers, who were Gentiles who believed in the God of the Jews, prayed to Him, and worshiped Him, but had not converted to Judaism. As far as a proud Jew was concerned, Gentiles were unclean, but proselytes and God-fearers were tolerated, with limitations. As God begins to prepare Peter for ministry among the Gentiles, who were considered unclean, it is mentioned three times that he was lodging at the home of Simon, a tanner (Acts 9:43; 10:6, 32). Tanning is the process by which animal skins are made usable for garments, tents, parchment, and other items. Under the Mosaic law, touching a dead thing made a person unclean.

Tanners were viewed as despised because of their uncleanness and the foul smell of their work. Therefore, a tanner would have been almost perpetually unclean. But Peter lodged with Simon, a tanner, for many days. Before we can be effective in ministering to people who are not like us, it helps to spend time with one person who is unlike us. Live among them and learn from them. This helps to prepare us for the next chapter, which is leading them or others like them to Christ. Live and learn; then lead.

Now therefore we are all here in the presence of
God to hear all that you have been commanded
by the Lord.(Acts 10:33)

As He exercises His divine wisdom and power, God has a way of working on both ends of a predetermined encounter between strangers that He will use to accomplish His will. Cornelius, a Roman centurion and God-fearer, is praying at 3:00 p.m. when an angel appears to him, and instructs him to send men to Joppa, and bring one Simon who is called Peter. The next day, Peter was praying at 12:00 p.m. and had a vision of all kinds of animals and reptiles and birds of the air. In Peter's vision, there were clean and unclean animals. The Jews followed strict dietary laws regarding the consumption of such animals. As Peter is entranced in this vision, a voice comes to him saying, "Rise, Peter, kill and eat." Peter has never eaten anything unholy or defiled, including the animals in this vision. The voice speaks again, saying, "What God has made clean, do not call common." Peter is now perplexed about the vision. The men who were sent by Cornelius arrived and asked for him. God was working with Cornelius in Caesarea while working with Peter in Joppa. He was working both ends and brought them together. Peter preached the gospel to Cornelius and his close relatives and friends. They believed and were saved. In the New Covenant, God not only ended dietary restrictions, He also broke down the wall of separation between Jews and Gentiles. Peter and Cornelius were men of prayer, and God spoke to them while they prayed. Prayer is not only preparation for the work; prayer is part of the work. Keep praying!

*He will declare to you a message by which
you will be saved, you and all your household.
(Acts 11:14)*

God is always working. He works through the power of His living Word, the Bible, and through the power of the Holy Spirit. He also works through human beings, saved and unsaved. He doesn't need us, nor do we deserve to participate on His kingdom agenda, but He chooses to use us in spite of us. God also uses His holy angels who are messengers sent from heaven. In Acts, chapter ten, God is working with Peter who is praying in Joppa. He shows Peter a vision of what the church should be, namely a spiritual organism that includes Jews and Gentiles. In Acts, chapter ten, God is also working with the Roman centurion, Cornelius, who is praying in Caesarea. He shows Cornelius a vision of an angel standing in his house saying, "Send to Joppa and bring Simon who is called Peter." The angel announces to Cornelius that Peter will declare to him a message by which he will be saved, as well as all his household. When Peter arrived, he preached the good news of peace through Jesus Christ. He preached the death, burial, and resurrection of Christ. Peter preached that after His resurrection, Christ showed Himself to those who had been chosen by God as witnesses, who ate and drank with Him after He rose from the dead. Peter preached to them that Christ is the one God has appointed as judge of the living and the dead. He preached that everyone who believes in Him receives forgiveness of sins through His name. Cornelius and his household were saved, filled with the Holy Spirit, and baptized.

God's work through His church is not that of duplicating earthly organizations. His work in and through the church is a saving, and sanctifying work. There is work that everyone can do. But there is a work that only the church can do, and it begins with a message that only the church can declare.

*Peter was sleeping between two soldiers, bound
with two chains, and sentries before the door
were guarding the prison. (Acts 12:6)*

The amazing thing about this verse of Scripture is that
the apostle Peter is sleeping. How can a man sleep in prison
while chained to the two soldiers who are guarding him? How
can a man sleep in prison knowing that a former business
partner, close confidant, brother in Christ, and fellow apostle
was arrested the day before and executed with the sword? How
can a man sleep in prison being fully aware of King Herod
Agrippa's intent to kill him as well? Well, Peter did confess on
one occasion that he was willing to go to prison and even die
with Jesus. Maybe it was because earnest prayer was made to
God for him by the church, but I really believe that Peter was
able to sleep at such a time as this because of the promise Jesus
made to him concerning his death. Jesus prophesied that Peter
would die by crucifixion as an old man (John 21:18–19). This
prophesy was spoken by Jesus in AD 33. The events of Acts,
chapter twelve, take place in AD 42, which is only nine years
later. Peter was still a young man, and King Herod planned to
have him executed by the sword, just as James, the brother of
John, was. I'm sure that the prayers of the church were helpful.
But I believe Peter was sleeping on the promise of Christ. If
God said it, it's settled. Now go to sleep.

And when the Gentiles heard this, they began
rejoicing and glorifying the word of the Lord.
(Acts 13:48)

The apostle Paul said on one occasion concerning the gospel, "It is the power of God for salvation to everyone who believes, to the Jew first and also to the Greek." Paul sometimes used the term *Greek* to refer to all Gentiles, and Gentiles were non-Jews. In the Old Testament, the Jews were God's chosen people, but they apparently forgot what they were chosen for. They were chosen as a nation to be a light for the Gentiles. When the Gentiles at Antioch heard this, according to The Message Bible, "They could hardly believe their good fortune." They began to rejoice and glorify (honor) the Word of the Lord. These non-Jews were rejoicing because salvation was available to them. And the availability of salvation was made known to them through the Word of the Lord. As a result, they were honoring the Word of the Lord. I repeat, they were honoring the Word of the Lord! Like those Gentiles, we should have a high view of the Word of the Lord. Those who were appointed to eternal life believed. They believed the Word of the Lord. Our belief system should not be based on unbiblical song lyrics, old wives' tales, and suspect theological interpretations. We should have such an appreciation for the Word of the Lord, that we are compelled to actually read it, rejoice in it, and honor it.

Strengthening the souls of the disciples, encouraging them to continue in the faith, and saying that through many tribulations we must enter the kingdom of God. (Acts 14:22)

Brothers and sisters in the faith need to be strengthened and encouraged from time to time. The rigors of the Christian life, which includes life in general, make it necessary. Anyone who says that living the Christian life is easy is either not a Christian or just being untruthful. The totality of life and all that it encompasses will sometimes wear us down. Life has its ebbs and flows, and we just need a spiritual pep talk periodically. In verse 2 of this chapter, unbelieving Jews in Iconium stirred up the Gentiles and poisoned their minds against the brothers. But they continued to boldly preach the gospel. In verse 5 of this chapter, an attempt was made to mistreat and stone them. They learned of it and fled to Lystra and Derbe but continued to preach the gospel. In verse 19, Jews came from Antioch and Iconium and persuaded the crowds to stone Paul. They dragged him out of the city because they thought he was dead. But God raised him, and he continued to preach the gospel. These believers were faithful to their calling. The Word was preached, and souls were saved, but there were many tribulations. With these experiences under their belt, they returned to the very places where these tribulations occurred, in hope that they would strengthen and encourage the souls of the disciples. They were trying to help somebody.

Now, therefore, why are you putting God to the test by placing a yoke on the necks of the disciples that neither our fathers nor we have been able to bear?(Acts 15:10)

Salvation is by grace alone, through faith alone, in Christ alone. No one is saved by keeping the Old Testament Law. The rite of circumcision in the Old Testament did not save anyone but was a means of identification, a sign of the covenant between God and Israel. The ordinance of baptism in the New Testament doesn't save anyone but is a means of identification, a sign of the union between Christ and those who are a part of His body, the church. As Gentiles began to hear and receive the gospel of Christ, there was much joy among the believers in Jerusalem. But certain Jews, known as the Judaizers, believed that Gentiles should be circumcised and obey the law of Moses to become bona fide Christians. In suggesting this, they were placing a yoke on the necks of Gentile disciples that Jews were never able to bear. This is not what God intended for believers, Jew or Gentile. The Old Testament law has 613 commandments and prohibitions, a yoke that no one can bear. Jesus lived a sinless life, thereby fulfilling the law. The gospel is the good news about the substitutionary death of Christ, and His subsequent burial and resurrection. Our faith in Him is what saves us. "For by grace you have been saved through faith. And this is not your own doing; it is the gift of God, not a result of works, so that no one may boast" (Eph. 2:8–9). There won't be any boasting in heaven about how we got there. We all get there the same way.

Having been forbidden by the Holy Spirit...but the Spirit of Jesus did not allow them...immediately we sought to go on into Macedonia, concluding that God had called us to preach the gospel to them. (Acts 16:6–10)

As born-again believers in Jesus Christ, we don't chart our own paths or set our own kingdom agendas. We are God's workmanship, and the good works that He would have us to do were previously prepared for us before the foundation of the world. Most of us have ventured into areas of ministry that were of our own choosing, only to discover that the will of God did not lead us there. It is even possible to be involved in the right ministry, and have a desire to labor in the wrong vineyard. This is where thanks and praises to God for the Holy Spirt are in order. The Holy Spirit is our helper, comforter, and teacher. He leads and guides us according to the will of God for our lives. The apostle Paul and his companions were forbidden by the Holy Spirit to speak the word in Asia. They attempted to go into Bithynia, but the Spirit of Jesus did not allow them. Many times, the doors that we want opened are closed and locked by God Himself. He closes doors that no one can open, and He opens doors that no one can close. When our spiritual eyes and ears are open, God will enable us to see, hear, and know which path to take. The pathway of duty is paved by the Lord, and He orders the steps of those who seek to do His will.

But now He commands all people everywhere
to repent, because He has fixed a day on which
He will judge the world in righteousness by a
Man whom He has appointed. (Acts 17:30–31)

John the Baptist began his ministry with the warning, "Repent, for the kingdom of heaven is at hand." After Jesus was baptized by John and tempted by the devil in the wilderness, He began to preach, saying, "Repent, for the kingdom of heaven is at hand." Repentance is a turning from sin and a turning to God. It is a changing of one's behavior as the result of changing one's mind about sin. God has commanded all people everywhere to repent. Repentance is necessary because "all have sinned and fall short of the glory of God." None of us have lived up to the divine standard, which is perfection. God will never lower the standard for righteousness. It is, has always been, and will always be perfection.

Repentance is also necessary because God has fixed a day on which He will judge the world in righteousness. His appointed judge is none other than our Lord and Savior Jesus Christ. The judge said on one occasion, "But unless you repent, you will all likewise perish" (Luke 13:3). The apostle Paul said, "For godly grief (sorrow) produces a repentance that leads to salvation without regret" (2 Cor. 7:10). This is the work of the Holy Spirit within the human heart that leads to salvation and spiritual growth. When we have turned from sin and turned to God, there is no fear of judgment. The judge is righteous, and He's our friend. What a friend we have in Jesus!

And when they opposed and reviled him, he shook out his garments and said to them, "Your blood be on your own heads! I am innocent" (Acts 18:6).

As we go about our lives worshiping God and working for Him, we must remember that we are also called to be His witnesses. We have seen, heard, and experienced the wonderful works of God, and it is His will that we bear witness to those who don't know Him. Those of us who know Christ have the responsibility of making Him known. Not everyone will accept or believe the good news that we share about Christ.

Some people will even oppose and revile us as we seek to fulfill the Master's mandate. No one ever spoke like Jesus, yet He was despised and rejected, mocked, and ridiculed, and eventually crucified. If the Lord Himself was rejected, we will experience rejection as well. Sometimes we have to throw up our hands after realizing that we're whipping a dead horse. We shouldn't cast our pearls before swine or give what is holy to the dogs. In Bible times, watchmen were stationed on city walls, keeping an eye out for approaching danger. If danger was approaching and the watchman failed to warn the people, their blood was on his hands. If the watchman warned the people, and they ignored him, their blood was on their own heads. The watchman was, therefore, innocent. We worship, work, witness, watch, warn, and wait in faith.

Paul has persuaded and turned away a great many people, saying that gods made with hands are not gods. (Acts 19:26)

Idolatry is the worship of something created as opposed to the Creator. Idolatry is sinful and demonic. Christian preachers are in the "turning" business, which is the business of persuading people to turn from the sinful and demonic, and turn to the one true living God. How foolish can a person be to think that something imagined in the mind of man, and made by the hands of man, is worthy of man's worship? The God of the Bible is omnipotent, omniscient, and omnipresent. He is all-powerful, all-knowing, and present everywhere at the same time, in all of His fullness. He does whatever He pleases. An idol is a lifeless impotent production of a sinful person's imagination, that cannot perform in any way. Idols cannot do anything. The faculties of idols do not function. They have eyes but cannot see. They have ears but cannot hear. They have mouths but cannot speak. They must be carried from one place to another. They do not respond to the prayers of those who petition them. Idolatry is the epitome of foolishness. Gods made with hands are not gods, period! The God of the Bible is eternal. From everlasting to everlasting, He is God. He is uncreated, has no beginning or ending, and is the cause and creator of all there is. We worship Him, and Him alone.

*For I did not shrink from declaring to you the
whole counsel of God. (Acts 20:27)*

Spiritual alertness within a congregation is of the
utmost importance, especially among the ranks of those in
leadership. Many churches have become open and accepting
to various kinds of false teaching and fail to see the damage
that is being done to the household of faith. Spiritual discernment seems to have been buried with the sages and elders of
yesteryear. There have always been external and internal forces
at work for the purpose of misleading the disciples of Christ.
Therefore, the apostle Paul admonishes us to be spiritually alert
and discerning when it comes to external and internal threats
against the Lord's church. The churches would benefit greatly if
pastors wouldn't avoid declaring to them the whole counsel of
God. There are numerous words that have been removed from
the vocabularies of Christian preachers, teachers, and leaders.
Many have become too concerned about seeker-sensitivity and
not offending anyone. As a result, the whole counsel of God
is exchanged for something more positive and entertaining.
Church attendees have become accustomed to a weekly dose of
a cross-less and Christ-less gospel. Whatever needs to be done
in and through the church is done by God's people, through
God's Word and God's Spirit. If these can't do it, it can't be done.

> *For I am ready not only to be imprisoned but even to die in Jerusalem for the name of the Lord Jesus. (Acts 21:13)*

The average believer is always ready for that which is comfortable, convenient, and cost-free. On the other hand, the apostle Paul was always ready to go where the Lord directed, and to do or be whatever the Lord desired. This kind of readiness defined his entire ministry. While in Tyre, the disciples told Paul "through the Spirit" not to go up to Jerusalem. But he was ready. While spending time in Caesarea with Philip the evangelist, a prophet by the name of Agabus took Paul's belt and bound his own hands and feet. After doing this, Agabus said, "Thus says the Holy Spirit, this is how the Jews at Jerusalem will bind the man who owns this belt." Paul was also warned by all the disciples who were present. But Paul was ready to be imprisoned and even to die at Jerusalem for the name of the Lord Jesus. After failing to dissuade him from going to Jerusalem, the disciples gave up and said, "Let the will of the Lord be done." In this situation, it appears as though Paul's readiness was contrary to the guidance given by the Holy Spirit. But in the previous chapter, Paul was told by the Spirit that bonds and afflictions awaited him. If Paul wanted to avoid afflictions and imprisonment, he wouldn't set foot in Jerusalem. But like his Master and Savior, he set his face toward Jerusalem. Paul said in chapter 20, "But I do not account my life of any value nor as precious to myself, if only I may finish my course and the ministry that I received from the Lord Jesus, to testify to the gospel of the grace of God." He did not choose that which was comfortable, convenient, and cost-free. He fought the good fight, finished the race, kept the faith, and anticipated his crown.

And one Ananias…came to me, and standing by
me said to me, "Brother Saul" (Acts 22:12-13).

Some words should be used with the utmost care and consideration. Words such as love, friend, and brother are among the most important in our vocabulary. Saul of Tarsus was probably the person most unlikely to be received as a brother by anyone in the church. After all. He was the one who guarded the coats of those who murdered Stephen and approved of his execution. He would later become a fierce persecutor of the church. But after his conversion on the Damascus Road, and having lost his eyesight, he was led into the city and waited for three days, praying in the dark. Jewish converts to Christianity were often disowned by their families. Some Jewish families would even have funerals for their loved ones who left Judaism for Christianity. But God always sends His people who and what they need.

Ananias was sent to Saul by God. Ananias had heard of Saul and was hesitant about going to him. But God assured him that Saul was a chosen vessel who would carry His name before Gentiles and kings and the children of Israel. Saul had seen a vision of a man named Ananias coming in and laying his hands on him so that he might regain his sight. Ananias came to him, stood by him, and called him brother. Brother is a word that's filled with profound and significant meaning. A brother will come to you, stand by you, and brother you. Christian men should be committed to brothering their brothers.

Now the son of Paul's sister heard of their ambush. (Acts 23:16)

As Christian believers who are committed to doing the Lord's will, we should never be surprised when hearing of the plots and plans of the enemy. Though the enemy is concerned about all believers, he is more aggressive toward those who pose a threat to his kingdom. Even though he is cunning and crafty, he does not possess the attributes of almighty God. Our God is omniscient, omnipotent, and omnipresent. Nothing can slip past His omniscience, overpower His omnipotence, or evade His omnipresence. He is God, and He has no equals. Even though God is always aware of the enemy's plans, He doesn't always reveal them to us. But sometimes He does. In the context of this passage, over forty Jews made a plot and bound themselves by an oath neither to eat nor drink till they killed Paul. Somehow God saw to it that Paul's nephew heard about it and reported it to Paul. Paul sent his nephew to the proper authorities so they would be aware of this ambush. In response to a previous attempt on Paul's life, God has him placed in protective custody. Now in response to the forty-plus men who have pledged to kill him, God has providentially blessed Paul with a 472-man security detail. If God is for us, who can be against us? In the words of the prophet Elisha, "Do not be afraid, for those who are with us are more than those who are with them" (2 Kings 6:16). God knows how to provide for and protect His own.

For we have found this man a plague. (Acts 24:5)

When God called and converted Saul of Tarsus, he was told from the very beginning how much he must suffer for the sake of the Lord's name. Prior to his conversion he was the predator, and all Christians were his prey. Now that God has begun His transforming work in him, he became the prey, and his countrymen the predators. The once respected, feared, and admired persecutor then was a preacher and defender of the faith he previously tried to exterminate. Because of his passionate preaching through the power of the Holy Spirit within him, Paul had become a pest to the Jewish religious establishment. They would have liked to see him imprisoned and even executed. As Paul stood before Governor Felix in Caesarea, Tertullus, his prosecutor says, "We have found this man a plague." The King James Version says, "a pestilent fellow." When you are about right and righteousness, the world will see you differently. To the world, you have become a fly to be swatted or a pest to be exterminated. Instead of the religious leaders allowing the Scriptures to speak to them, they chose to label the Lord's messenger as a troublemaker. Because of his influence and the effectiveness of his ministry, he was considered a public menace, a mischievous and malignant person. But Paul was in good company; and so are we when we stir up good trouble. The rotten King Ahab called the prophet Elijah, "O troubler of Israel." The truth of the Word does not change.

Let them call us whatever they will.

*A certain Jesus, who was dead, but whom Paul
asserted to be alive. (Acts 25:19)*

Once while taking a class, the instructor who was a
pastor mentioned to us that his church had an upcoming business meeting. He stated that he knew there would be people in
attendance who were not in favor of what he would be recom-
mending to the church. He shared with us that he stated to the
members of the congregation, "If you're coming to the meeting
to fight, be sure to bring your Bibles." Some people fight and
resist because they are just plain evil. Others fight and resist
because they are ignorant of God's Word. And there are those
who fight and resist because they are evil and ignorant. The
enemies of the apostle Paul were ignorant and evil. They were
not ignorant in the sense of being uneducated. They were ignorant of the prophecies concerning Jesus because their knowledge of the Jews' religion was simply academic, social, and
political. God's Word had not been internalized and applied to
their hearts. These religious leaders constantly plotted against
Paul and sought to take his life because He was preaching Jesus.
Jesus is Lord and Savior. He did die on the cross at Calvary, but
God raised Him from the dead on the third day. Among Paul's
enemies were the Sadducees who did not believe in the resurrection of the dead and only accepted the Pentateuch, a term
applied to the first five books of the Bible. The Pharisees were
also enemies of Paul. They did believe in the resurrection but
ignored so much more. Either we believe the Bible or we don't.
True Christian believers don't pick and choose which parts of
the Bible we are going to believe and live by. We believe all of
it or none of it.

Why is it thought incredible by any of you that
God raises the dead? (Acts 26:8)

The hope of every Christian believer is to be caught up together with those who have died in Christ at His coming. Not only this, but every believer dies with the hope of being raised from the dead and receiving a glorified body when the Lord returns. The hope of the resurrection is not something that came into existence in the New Testament with the church age. The Old Testament saints lived with this same hope. The patriarch Job said, "For I know that my Redeemer lives...And after my skin has been destroyed, yet in my flesh I shall see God, whom I shall see for myself, and my eyes shall behold, and not another" (Job 19:25-27). David said, "For You will not abandon my soul to Sheol, or let Your holy one (Christ) see corruption (decay)" (Ps. 16:10). The prophet Isaiah said, "Your dead shall live; their bodies shall rise. You who dwell in the dust, awake and sing for joy!...and the earth will give birth to the dead" (Isa. 26:19). The patriarchs, prophets, and kings looked forward to the resurrection of the dead. By the power of God, prophets, apostles, and Jesus Himself raised the dead; but those who were raised eventually died again. Jesus is the first begotten from the dead, which means that He is the first to be raised from the dead, never to die again. This truth gives us the assurance of our own resurrection.

Why would anyone with this knowledge think of this as something not to be believed?

The God to whom I belong and whom I worship.
(Acts 27:23)

For the born-again believer in Christ, there is no question about to whom we belong, or whom we worship. We worship God almighty, the Creator of heaven and earth and all there is. Even during tempestuous and tumultuous times, we know to whom we belong and whom we worship. The apostle Paul was now a prisoner among prisoners, onboard a ship headed for Rome. All he has done since his Damascus Road experience is worship and serve God, yet he found himself out on the stormy sea. Sometimes God will allow the winds to blow in the lives of those who belong to Him and worship Him. In Acts 27, "wind" is mentioned five times. Dr. Luke, the author of Acts, says, "The winds were against us; The wind did not allow us to go farther; Now when the south wind blew gently; But soon a tempestuous wind, called the northeaster, struck down from the land; And when the ship was caught and could not face the wind, we gave way to it and were driven along." The wind was the reason they were violently storm-tossed. The prophet Nahum said, "His way is in whirlwind and storm, and the clouds are the dust of His feet" (Nah. 1:3). Our souls are anchored in the Lord. He has the power to speak to wind and waves: Peace! Be still!

There we found brothers...And the brothers there...On seeing them, Paul thanked God and took courage. (Acts 28:14–15)

As far as we know, Luke and Aristarchus of Thessalonica were the only Christian brothers who traveled with Paul on his journey to Rome. However, the Lord was with him as he endured this stormy season of his life. The only person we really need in life is God; and He'll provide companions, friends, and brothers and sisters. But in the absence of Christian brothers and sisters, God will sometimes move unbelievers to show kindness and generosity toward His children. After Paul was shipwrecked on Malta, the soldiers were planning to kill all of the prisoners. But Julius, the centurion who was assigned to Paul, kept them from carrying out their plan. While on Malta, the native people welcomed them and showed unusual kindness to them. The chief man of the island received them and entertained them hospitably for three days. During their stay there, they were honored, and everything they needed was put on board the ship before their departure. But when they arrived in Puteoli they found brothers and sisters who invited them to stay seven days. Finally, people of like precious faith! When they arrived in Rome, brothers and sisters came to them. On seeing them, Paul thanked God and took courage. Sometimes all the encouragement we need is found in seeing our brothers and sisters in Christ. For this we thank God. Hold on saints!

*Paul, a servant of Christ Jesus, called to be
an apostle, set apart for the gospel of God.
(Rom. 1:1)*

In the opening words of Paul's greeting to the church at
Rome, he makes mention of three things that apply to every
born-again believer. He refers to himself as a "servant" of Christ
Jesus. In this usage, Paul considers himself a slave, a person
owned as the possession of another. He realized that he was
bought at a price and was not his own. The slave relinquishes
his will and concerns himself with the will of his master. So it
is with us; "Not my will, but Your will be done," Oh Lord. Paul
also says that he was "called." Every child of God is called to
salvation. We were chosen in Christ before the foundation of
the world. We did not choose Him; He chose us. Inherent in
the call to salvation is the call to a particular area of ministry.
For Paul, it was the call to apostleship. We should be sure of our
calling and be faithful in the same. Like Paul, every believer is
"set apart" (sanctified). We are set apart from the world to God
to be used by Him. The One who loves us and saved us has
made possible the reality of fellowship with Him. From beginning to end, it's all about us being in fellowship with Him as
servants, exercising our calling, and growing in the grace and
knowledge of Him.

*That we may be mutually encouraged by each
other's faith, both yours and mine. (Rom. 1:12)*

What a wonderful picture of mutual encouragement! Paul
the apostle points out that every born-again believer is loved
by God. We impart to others what God has imparted to us.
The love of God has been shed abroad in our hearts; therefore,
we have a mutual love for one another. Jesus prayed for all
believers; therefore, we exercise mutual intercession for one
another. Our hope of seeing other believers should be accompanied by a genuine desire to mutually encourage one another
by our faith. Don't forget that the one who ministers to you
and encourages you needs to be encouraged by you. Paul is
thankful to God because the faith of the Roman Christians is
proclaimed in all the world. Now he wants to have personal
fellowship with them that he may strengthen them and be
strengthened by them.

To those who by patience in well-doing seek for
glory and honor and immortality, He will give
eternal life. (Rom. 2:7)

Everyone who knows God through faith in Jesus Christ
has certain things in common. We have the joy of our common
salvation and all of the spiritual blessings that accompany it.
We are forever thankful for the forgiveness of sin and freedom
from guilt and condemnation. We appreciate God's grace and
mercy, and live in constant awareness of both. But there is also
the area of practical Christian living. Those who know and
love God are patient in well-doing. Those who are truly saved
practice obedient godly living, even though they may fail sometimes. Because of the fallen world in which we live and the
inner conflict between the flesh and Spirit, it requires endurance to not become weary in well-doing. The Bible does say that
we will reap if we do not give up. In a world where most people
seek glory and honor from people, we patiently endure because
we are pursuing the glory and honor that comes from God.
God's favorable opinion of His children is true glory, and the
eternal rewards that He will give us are genuine honor. When
the Lord comes, we will take off mortality and put on immortality. These are the things we seek, and they all accompany
eternal life.

For all have sinned and fall short of the glory of God. (Rom. 3:23)

Every human being is born with the propensity to sin. This is because of the sin-nature we inherited from the first man, Adam. All have sinned (past tense). And all fall short of the glory of God (present tense). This is true of every one of us. We have sinned, and we fall short—period! Even though people continue to define sin on their own terms and according to their personal beliefs, sin is still what God says it is. All sin is not the same, but all unrighteousness is sin. Sin is missing the mark, which is failing to live perfectly no matter how hard we try. Sin is trespassing or transgressing, which means to overstep a forbidden line. Sin is iniquity, that which is inwardly crooked and perverse. Sin is abomination, that which is detestable and abhorrent in the eyes of God. Sin is just as bad as it sounds and is even worse. Sin is the reason we needed the Savior. The Savior is the one who saves, delivers, and forgives. Sin is the reason God sent Jesus. Sin is the reason Jesus died on His cross. Sin is the reason God raised Jesus from the dead for our justification (right legal standing before God). If we confess our sins, He is faithful and just to forgive us our sins and to cleanse us from all unrighteousness. (1 John 1:9) The Holy Spirit shows us our sin, then He shows us the Savior.

But the words "it was counted to him" were not written for his sake alone, but for ours also. (Rom. 4:23–24)

Abraham is not only the father of the Jewish nation, he is also the father of all those who believe, meaning, all who have trusted Christ for salvation. Abraham was justified (counted as righteous) by faith. The Bible teaches that Abraham *believed* God, and it was counted to him as righteousness. If Abraham was justified by works, he would have something to boast about. But when we get to heaven, we won't hear Abraham or anyone else boasting about how they got there. All are saved by grace alone, through faith alone, in Christ alone. God justifies (counts as righteous) the ungodly when they believe Him; this is when the ungodly become children of God. This biblical truth was written for our sake. It's good to know that regardless of our sinful past, God's saving grace is still in effect. Abraham was counted as righteous before he was circumcised. Circumcision was a sign of the righteousness which had been credited to him by faith while he was uncircumcised. For us, baptism is the sign of the righteousness which was credited to us by faith before we were baptized. God took our sin and placed it on Jesus; He took Jesus's righteousness and placed it on us. How we thank God for salvation by grace through faith!

But God shows His love for us in that while we
were still sinners, Christ died for us. (Rom. 5:8)

Even with our limited wisdom, understanding, and insight, God is concerned about us seeing things from heaven's point of view. Therefore, He sometimes puts these things on display. Psalm 19:1 says, "The heavens declare the glory of God, and the sky above proclaims His handiwork." He often displays His wisdom and power. In Psalm 139, David says, "O LORD, You have searched me and known me! You know when I sit down and when I rise up; You discern my thoughts from afar." In Exodus chapter 14, the Lord drove the sea back by a strong east wind all night and made the sea dry land, and the waters were divided. These were demonstrations of His wisdom and power. But God also demonstrates His love for us. Jesus came into this world because of the love His Father has for us. For God so loved the world that He gave His one and only Son. The love that God demonstrates is "His own" love. Many people demonstrate counterfeit and phony love. But because God is love, He exhibits His own genuine love. God displays His love just as merchants display merchandise for the interested customer. But God isn't selling anything; He is the original Giver; the giver of every good and perfect gift. The cross of Christ was God's love on display. While we were sinners, Christ died for us. That's love!

For the wages of sin is death, but the free gift
of God is eternal life in Christ Jesus our Lord.
(Rom. 6:23)

I would rather receive the free gift that comes from God than the wages of sin that I've earned. One of the things I love and appreciate about God's free gift is the fact that it includes many free "gifts." In the previous chapter, the apostle mentions the *free gift* five times. It's amazing when we realize that the *free gift* of grace makes the *free gift* of eternal life possible, and the *free gift* of eternal life provides even more grace. The *free gift* of eternal life also bestows upon us the *free gift* of justification. Justification is right legal standing before God. When we receive the *free gift* of eternal life we can say, "Because I am justified, God looks at me just-if-I'd (justified) never sinned; and it's a free gift. Finally, the *free gift* of eternal life also provides the *free gift* of righteousness. There are still those among us who are ignorant of God's righteousness and go about attempting to establish a righteousness of their own. Christ is the end of the law for righteousness to everyone who believes. (Rom. 10:4) Any attempt at a self-imposed righteousness will result in wages instead of God's gracious gift that bestows many gifts. Anyone who has sanctified common sense doesn't want what they have earned; they want God's free gift.

Yet if it had not been for the law, I would not have known sin. (Rom. 7:7)

A nation needs laws and people need to be governed by them. Without laws, there is no standard of right and wrong in society. The only way to insure or promote civility, order, and accountability in society is through laws. Without laws we welcome chaos, confusion, and disorder. When God was establishing Israel as a nation and as a people, He gave to them the Law through Moses. But God knew in His omniscience that no one would be able to perfectly keep the 613 commandments and prohibitions found in the law. But one of the reasons the law was given to Israel was to make their sin known to them. The apostle Paul says, "If it had not been for the law, I would not have known sin" (Rom. 7:7). This is the purpose of the law, to create in lost sinners a sense of guilt and need. The law shows us how we so desperately need the Savior. The law was given through Moses; grace and truth came through Jesus Christ. (John 1:17) The law has fulfilled its purpose. We know that we were sinners in need of a Savior, and the Savior has done what the law could not do. Let us be ever mindful of the grace of God.

He foreknew...predestined...conformed...called...
justified...glorified. (Rom. 8:29–30)

This happens to be one of my favorite passages in all of the Bible. It follows my favorite verse in the Bible which is Romans 8:28. This passage is my favorite because it assures me of my eternal security. Other passages give the same assurance, but this one is my favorite. God foreknew us. Before the foundation of the world, God knew who would be saved. It is also implied that just as God knew Jeremiah before he was formed in the womb, He also knew us. In the mind of God, the relationship already existed. God also predestined us to be conformed to the image of His Son.

This speaks of the sanctification process from beginning to end; from being nothing like Jesus to seeing Him as He is and being like Him in heaven. Whom He foreknew, predestined, and conformed, He also called. This is the effectual call to salvation, to follow Him and be His disciple. Those of us who responded to the call to salvation have been justified; therefore, we have right legal standing before God. Justification is an irreversible legal decision; therefore, we are saved and safe. Whom He justified He also glorified. Glorification is the final state of the redeemed. God sees our salvation from foreknowledge all the way to glorification. Every action by God mentioned in this passage is in the past tense, as though it had already happened. In the mind of God, our salvation is a done deal. This assurance will make the rest of your earthly existence more joyful, peaceful, and hopeful. Now run on and see what the end is going to be.

> *As it is written, "Behold, I am laying in Zion a stone of stumbling, and a rock of offense; and whoever believes in Him will not be put to shame" (Rom. 9:33).*

God does not concern Himself with meeting our expectations. He is concerned about His will, His purposes, His promises, and His decrees. Many times what we are looking for with great expectation is not what God is sending to us. And if we are not careful, it is possible that we may totally miss what God is saying and doing. This is what happened to God's chosen people, the Jews. They were aware of the fact that God was going to send the Messiah. But the majority totally missed Him when He came because He did not live or perform according to their expectations. They were offended by His humility and compassion. When they challenged Him from a religious standpoint. He poked holes in their theology. His enemies did not approve of the company He kept, and even accused Him of being demon-possessed.

What they did not realize and could not comprehend because of their spiritual blindness was that God was building a spiritual house, and Jesus was the chief cornerstone. Whoever believes in Him will not be put to shame. Do you believe this?

But how are they to call...How are they to believe...How are they to hear...And how are they to preach? (Rom. 10:14–15)

The gospel is the good news about the death, burial, and resurrection of our Lord and Savior Jesus Christ. The gospel is really the best news we will ever hear in our lives. The gospel is the good news and the best news because of its implications in this life and the life to come. The gospel message is the only saving message. Israel needed the gospel message. Paul's heart's desire and prayer to God for Israel was that they might be saved. Israel needed the gospel message, and the world needs the gospel message. People cannot be saved unless they call on the name of the Lord. For everyone who calls on the name of the Lord will be saved. But they cannot call on Him unless they believe with the heart. This means much more than giving mental assent to facts about Jesus; it means believing with the entire inner self, affecting the mind, emotions, and will. In order for one to believe. they must hear the word concerning Christ. Faith comes from hearing, and hearing through the word of Christ. The word of Christ is given to them by someone preaching the gospel message; the message of Christ and His cross. But God must call and send the preacher. All of God's preachers say the same things. They may have a different way of saying them, but they all say the same things. God is still extending His hands to disobedient and contrary people through the preaching of the gospel.

So too at the present time there is a remnant,
chosen by grace. (Rom. 11:5)

The Bible frequently speaks of a *remnant* in various contexts. What is common in each context is that it refers to "something left over." The term came to be applied specifically to the survival of a righteous few among the Jews who have been kept to form the nucleus of a new community of faith. The survival of a righteous remnant rests solely on God's providential care for His chosen people and His faithfulness to keep His covenant promises. The apostle Paul highlighted this concept to explain that the true Israel consists of Jews who believe in Christ and are part of His body, the church. This is the remnant that Paul speaks of. They are chosen by grace, which is God's unmerited favor. It has absolutely nothing to do with the keeping of the Old Testament law. African Americans in this nation have much in common with the Jews. We have been through similar trials and tribulations, and the Lord delivered us out of them all. In this country, there seems to be only a remnant of the African American church of old. Many have fallen away, and others have fallen for a Christ-less and cross-less pseudo-Christianity that cannot deliver on its promises. My heart's desire and prayer to God for African Americans is that they may be saved.

But be transformed by the renewal of your mind.
(Rom. 12:2)

In order for one's life to be transformed, the mind must be renewed. An old unspiritual way of thinking is what keeps people in the same rut their entire lives. This is what life becomes and continues to be when the mind is never renewed. Those who fail to heed the exhortation to renew their minds are sleep-walking and living like the walking dead. My mother had an expression that she would often use for someone who was lazy and trifling, and who lacked any hint of get-up-and-go. She would say, "He walks like life is falling off of him." This is the spiritual condition of those who refuse to renew their minds so that their lives may be transformed. A person will never rise above their own thinking, and our living is determined by our thinking. As a matter of biblical fact, every born-again child of God was predestined to be conformed to the image of Christ. This is a picture of sanctification, God's process of spiritual growth and development. This process flows as a result of the mind being renewed by the Word of God and the Spirit of God, who enables us to wise-up to the Word. Let us submit ourselves to the Word and Spirit of God.

Renew your mind and transform your life.

For salvation is nearer to us now than when we first believed. (Rom. 13:11)

Even though every born-again believer is completely and eternally saved, the salvation *experience* won't be fully actualized, realized, and appreciated until it has reached its ultimate state. Now remember, I am referring to our *experience* of salvation. The apostle Paul is telling the saints at Rome (and us) that salvation is *nearer* to us now than when we first believed. This is the explanation. Salvation is in three tenses: instantaneous salvation, continuing salvation, and ultimate salvation. In instantaneous salvation the believer *has been saved* from the guilt and penalty of sin and is safe. This happens instantly at the very moment we receive Christ by faith. This is called justification. In continuing salvation, the believer *is being saved* from the habit and dominion of sin. This is growing in grace, knowledge, and service of and for Christ. This process is called sanctification. In ultimate salvation, the believer *is to be saved* in the sense of entire conformity to Christ; sinless perfection. This *is to be saved* from the very presence of sin. This is called glorification. We know the time in which we are living, and the hour has come for us to wake from our spiritual slumber. Jesus is coming back just as He said He would.

It is good not to eat meat or drink wine or do anything that causes your brother to stumble. (Rom. 14:21)

There are many signs of spiritual maturity and immaturity. The person who is inconsiderate of other believers and demands their right to do certain things is an immature believer. The person who gives up their right to do certain things out of consideration for other believers is a mature believer. Because Christianity is not about rules and regulations, many believers think that it is okay to flaunt the liberty that we have in Christ. This is why so many believers frequent casinos, bars, parties, concerts, and other places where questionable behavior takes place. There are others who have no problem consuming alcoholic beverages in restaurants and other public settings. It also matters what kind of music we listen to and promote in the presence of others. I'm just saying! These are all signs of spiritual immaturity, and the one who engages in these kinds of activities are inconsiderate of other believers as well as unbelievers. In all that we do, we must be careful not to cause our brothers and sisters to stumble. We should also be considerate of unbelievers because we don't want our behavior to hinder them from coming to Christ. This is part of the self-denial that Jesus demanded of those who would follow Him. Our activities that are not sinful can become sin when we are inconsiderate of others and cause them to be offended. Mature believers are selfless, not selfish.

For whatever was written in former days was written for our instruction, that through endurance and through the encouragement of the Scriptures we might have hope. (Rom. 15:4)

Hope is expectant waiting; the constant expectation of a favorable outcome. Without hope we die; but as long as we have life we have hope. The born-again believer in Jesus Christ has been given new life in Him, therefore, there is always hope. What is the basis of the Christian's hope? We are reminded that what was written in the Old Testament was written for our instruction. Reading and meditating on the Old Testament Scriptures provide tremendous spiritual benefits to the child of God. Remember, the apostle Paul said, "All Scripture is breathed out by God and profitable" (2 Tim. 3:15). Paul encouraged Timothy to continue in what he had learned and firmly believed. From childhood, Timothy had been acquainted with the sacred writings, which are able to make one wise for salvation through Jesus Christ. (2 Tim.3:14-15) These sacred writings were the thirty-nine books (scrolls) of the Old Testament. The psalmist writes in 119:81, "I hope in Your word." The Christian hope is not founded in philosophy. One professor said, "Philosophy is a pile of mental mess." The Christian hope is not founded in New Age thought. This would be standing in sinking sand. When we have been instructed in the Word of God, we endure and persevere in it by the power of the Holy Spirit. And whenever a word of encouragement is needed, we turn to the Scriptures again and again. The Word of God is what gives us hope—the Old Testament and the New Testament.

Greet also the church in their house. (Rom. 16:5)

How is the spiritual health of the church that meets in your house? When the church was in the days of its infancy, believers sometimes met in homes that were large enough to accommodate the worship service attendees. These were house-churches. The homeowner wasn't necessarily the pastor; he was just someone who opened his heart to the Lord and opened his doors so the Lord's people would have a place to worship, fellowship, learn, and grow. If the home was owned by a husband and wife, they were not co-pastors of that congregation. They simply offered their place of residence as a place of worship for the local congregation. But how is the spiritual health of the church that meets in your house? The church that the apostle Paul greets in this verse met in the home of Priscilla and Aquila. They were not pastors or co-pastors, but they were Paul's fellow workers in Christ Jesus. Do you not know that we can be workers for Christ in our own homes? Absent of position or title, we are equipped to work in and for Him right there in our homes. Many believers are trying to save the community, city, and world, as their homes go to hell. The health of the church in your house is directly related to the spiritual health of the homeowner. Priscilla and Aquila (the homeowners) had risked their own necks for Paul's life. Sharing in the sufferings of another often begins after we lay ourselves on the line in support of them. This is when the reproaches that fall on them begin to fall on us. Lay it all on the line for those who share an address with you, and share in their sufferings. Having this kind of courageous character contributes to the spiritual health of the church in our homes. Believers of this caliber are worthy of our thanks. God won't say thanks, but He will say well done!

Who will sustain you to the end, guiltless in the
day of our Lord Jesus Christ. (1 Cor. 1:8)

As born-again believers in our Lord Jesus Christ, we are eagerly awaiting His return to rapture the redeemed from the earth. We are ever mindful of the promises made concerning His return. As Jesus ascended into heaven after His resurrection, two angelic messengers said to the apostles, "Men of Galilee, why do you stand looking into heaven? This Jesus, who was taken up from you into heaven, will come in the same way as you saw Him go into heaven" (Acts 1:11). This angelic announcement tells us at least two things: Jesus is in heaven, and He will return. Until He returns, we are being sustained by Him. Certainly He will supply every need of yours according to His riches in glory. But in this context, to be sustained by Him refers to His confirmation of our salvation and preservation in Him. No one can snatch us out of His hand. Our God is reliable, and this truth should inspire God-confidence and strengthen us during difficult times, knowing that we are eternally secure in Him. We are also encouraged by the truth that when He returns, we will be free from any legal charges against us. We will be blameless and unaccusable; the effects of justification. So we eagerly await His return, knowing that we are completely and eternally saved, and that our sins have been cast into the sea of forgetfulness where God has posted a "NO FISHING" sign.

But we have the mind of Christ. (1 Cor. 2:16)

To have the mind of Christ is to see things from heaven's point of view. The children of God should have minds that are saturated with the Word of God and illuminated by the Spirit of God. By way of His Word and His Spirit, God has granted to all of His children the capacity to know and understand His thoughts, although in a limited sense. The wisdom that God imparts to believers is not the wisdom of this age. There is, and should be, an emphasis on the secular education of the mind. A quality education enables us to become well rounded and informed individuals. But in the words of one songwriter, we are "living this life to live again." There is much more to life than the secular, the trivial, and the temporal. As children of God, even as we grapple with the everydayness of life, we desperately need to see things from heaven's point of view. People are who they are and know what they know as a result of their environment and what their minds have been exposed to. I often say that in order for a person's life to be transformed, their mind must be renewed. This Spirit and Word–induced renewal enables the believer to exercise discernment and understand more and more of the mind and will of God.

God is acquainted with all of our ways, and He knows our thoughts from afar. Let us become acquainted with His ways and able to discern His thoughts. It's all recorded in His self-disclosure, the Bible. One of the best things you could ever say to an author is, "I've read your book, and it transformed my life."

*So neither he who plants nor he who waters is
anything, but only God who gives the growth.
(1 Cor. 3:7)*

Two of the driving factors of disunity and sectarianism in
the church are spiritual immaturity and carnality. The apostle
Paul writes to the church at Corinth around AD 55. This is five
years after the Corinthian congregation was established. When
Paul came to them, he had to feed them with milk because
they were not ready for solid food. Five years had passed, and
he still had to speak to them as carnal-minded people rather
than spiritual-minded people. Because of their spiritual immaturity and their carnality, they were divided over the ministers
who preached the gospel to them. We can be sure that Paul
and Apollos had nothing to do with this factionalism in the
Corinthian church. As he writes under the inspiration of the
Holy Spirit, Paul confronts this childish behavior. The spiritual
"babes" in Corinth were quarreling about which preacher was
the greatest. Some preferred Paul, others chose Apollos, and
others favored Peter. This juvenile behavior produced three
congregations within the one. Children and childish adults love
to have debates about their heroes, even when their heroes are
ministers. Paul makes it clear that believers are to align themselves with the Lord, not their hero preacher. Preachers plant
and water, but only God can give life and growth. Don't miss
the forest while staring at one tree.

What do you have that you did not receive? If then you received it, why do you boast as if you did not receive it? (1 Cor. 4:7)

On a personal note, I thank God every day for saving me and using me. I also thank Him daily for using me in spite of myself. I realize that God doesn't need me but chooses to use me. I understand that I am not worthy to serve on His kingdom agenda. But I thank Him for making use of me anyhow. However, there are those who think more highly of themselves than they ought to think. Some people actually believe that God uses them because they bring so much to the table. In their way of thinking, they are really head and shoulders above everyone else, and this makes them special. These are those individuals who have an attitude of entitlement and superiority. They believe that they have earned the right to occupy lofty positions in God's church and don't mind speaking of their own worth and worthiness. People of this mindset also have a habit of looking down on those whom they consider unworthy and undeserving. After all, in their thinking, they are doing God and His church a favor because they have so much to offer. Well, they need to come back down to earth. The apostle Paul asked, "What do you have that you did not receive?" The answer is, nothing. He then asked, "If then you received it, why do you boast as if you did not receive it?" God gives to all mankind life and breath and everything.(Acts 17:25) In Him we live and move and have our being. (Acts 17:28) We have nothing to boast about. God is the first and last Giver. Whatever He has given us should be received with thanksgiving and humility, and used in His service with fear and trembling.

For what have I to do with judging outsiders?
Is it not those inside the church whom you are
to judge? God judges those outside. Purge the
evil person from among you. (1 Cor. 5:12–13)

A few days ago I watched a group of church leaders participate in a panel discussion that focused on perversion in the church. The panelists mainly discussed the origin and reality of perversion in the church. It was agreed upon by the panelists that perversion is a topic that many pastors avoid and refuse to preach or teach on. When the question arose about how perversion in the church should be dealt with, it was suggested that teaching and love were the answers. But these two are only part of the solution. What was interesting and disappointing to me was that there was no mention of accountability and church discipline. Certainly we all sin, but the church has a responsibility to hold its members accountable. Sin that is practiced openly and without shame should not be tolerated in the church. When we allow open and blatant sin to run rampant in the church, it ceases to be salt and light in a dark and decaying world.

The apostle Paul says that a little leaven permeates the entire lump. When sin in the church is ignored and swept under the rug, it spreads like wildfire. We are commanded by the Word of God to speak the truth in love. But we are also commanded by the Word of God to remove those individuals from the fellowship who are unrepentant when confronted about their sin. The church at Corinth wasn't willing to confront the known perversion among them and was rebuked by the apostle. What would he say to the churches of our day? When necessary, church discipline should be exercised out of love for the Lord, His people, and His church. And the ultimate goal is repentance, forgiveness, and restoration.

You are not your own, for you were bought with a price. So glorify God in your body. (1 Cor. 6:19–20)

How are you managing yourself? Every child of God is a steward, and a steward is one who manages the affairs and property of another. Stewardship is nothing less than a complete lifestyle, total accountability and responsibility before God. The Scripture is clear; you are not your own; you were bought with a price; so glorify God in your body. Christian stewardship begins with the management of one's self. Before one can become a faithful steward of the "things" God has entrusted to him, he must first surrender his entire self to God. We must present our "bodies" as living sacrifices to God. Any sacrifice made to God must pass divine inspection before it can be accepted. When we present our bodies to God, we are simply giving to Him what is already His. The entire self belongs to God: body and spirit/soul; the material and immaterial you. We have no right to do what we want with our bodies. The only right you have as a child of God is to do the will of God. The faithful steward is keenly aware of the fact that he does not belong to himself, but to God. Therefore, faithful stewards seek to glorify God in body and spirit. The faithful steward strives to live a life that honors Christ our Savior. How are you managing yourself? If you have done well, you will hear, "Well done!" If you have not done well, then oh well.

But because of the temptation to sexual immorality, each man should have his own wife and each woman her own husband. (1 Cor. 7:2)

Contrary to popular opinion and cultural acceptance, sexual immorality is defined as any sexual activity outside of the marriage relationship between a man and a woman. Adultery is a form of sexual immorality. Homosexuality is a form of sexual immorality. Even sexual involvement between heterosexuals is considered sexual immorality if the parties are not married to each other. And there are other kinds of sexual immorality. Even though God created us as sexual beings, marriage is His only provision for sexual fulfillment. For Christians like the apostle Paul, who have the gift of celibacy, this is not a personal issue. But for the majority of believers, passionate desires must be managed. If one is single and cannot exercise self-control, they should marry. For it is better to marry than to be aflame with passion. (1 Cor. 7:9) The purposes of marriage are procreation, companionship, and avoiding sexual immorality. For those who don't possess the gift of celibacy, sexual temptation is a clear and present danger. Because of this temptation, each man should have his own wife, and each woman her own husband. Until that time comes, God is able to keep those who desire to be kept, even if you have to occasionally flee.

So run that you may obtain it. (1 Cor. 9:24)

Serious athletes understand the importance and necessity of self-control and a disciplined lifestyle. Their seriousness can be seen in the way they take care of themselves. Physical training and preparation is most important. A restricted and healthy diet is required. And allowing the body to rest and recharge is of the utmost importance. All of these measures are taken so that the committed athlete may be best prepared to win the desired prize. The disciplined life of the determined athlete is an illustration of the Christian life. The believer is not running the Christian race to get to heaven. The matter of our salvation is settled forever. We are running to live the victorious Christian life, to win souls to Christ, and to obtain a prize at the Lord's coming.

Everything that we are pursuing has eternal significance. Therefore, like the disciplined athlete, we bring our entire being into subjection in order that we might obtain the nonperishable prize. It takes effort, dedication, and discipline to win at anything. Claiming and decreeing oneself to be a winner is not what winning athletes do. They put in the work, learn from experience, seek the wisdom of the elders, and stick to a proven regimen. The victorious Christian life requires the same. Let us also lay aside every weight, and sin which clings so closely, and let us run with endurance the race that is set before us, looking to Jesus, the founder and perfecter of our faith. (Heb. 12:1-2)

(Now these things took place as examples for us, that we might not desire evil as they did. (1 Cor. 10:6)

The children of Israel's journey from Egypt to the Promised Land serves as a reminder of the dangers and consequences of unbelief and evil desire. They were all under the cloud and passed through the sea.

They all ate the same spiritual food and drank the same spiritual drink. They all drank from the same spiritual Rock which was Christ. Like us, they were all participants of the same fellowship. But it was more outward than inward. The first ten verses of this chapter are filled with examples of cause and effect.

With most of the Israelites, God was not pleased (cause). And they were overthrown in the wilderness (effect). They were guilty of idolatry and sexual immorality (cause). As a result, twenty-three thousand fell in one day (effect). They put Christ to the test by questioning His plan and purpose, even though He was providing for and protecting them (cause). Because of this, they were destroyed by serpents (effect). The children of Israel constantly murmured, grumbled, and complained (cause). For this reason they were destroyed by the destroyer, who was an angel of death sent by God (effect). Now these things happened to them as an example, but they were written down for our instruction. Let us read the writings and avoid the pitfalls of the children of Israel who failed to enter the Promised Land.

But if we judged ourselves truly, we would not be judged. (1 Cor. 11:31)

There are three kinds of judgment for the child of God: church judgment, divine judgment, and self-judgment. Church judgment comes into play when members of a local congregation refuse to repent of their publicly known sin. The local church has the responsibility to "judge" by removing the unrepentant individual from the fellowship (1 Cor. 5:2). Divine judgment (chastening) also takes place when the child of God is unrepentant and refuses to properly judge their own sin. We are given examples of divine judgment in verse 30, which states, "That is why many of you are weak and ill, and some have died." When we are judged by the Lord, we are disciplined by Him so that we may not be condemned along with the world (1 Cor. 11:32). There is also self-judgment. Church judgment and divine judgment can be avoided by properly judging ourselves. God forgives us when we acknowledge, confess, and repent of our sin.

This is what it means to properly or truly judge ourselves. The apostle Paul gives this exhortation in the context of partaking of the Lord's Supper in an unworthy manner, which is a sin. But it applies to any sin in our lives. Sin is whatever the Word of God says it is. Judge yourself by acknowledging it, confessing it, and repenting of it. Anyone who has sanctified common sense would prefer self-judgment over church or divine judgment.

All these are empowered by one and the same
Spirit, who apportions to each one individually
as He wills. (1 Cor. 12:11)

A spiritual gift is a special ability given by the Holy Spirit to believers, to be used to minister to others in order to build up the church, the body of Christ. In order for the local church to function at maximum effectiveness, each member must be involved in a ministry that utilizes their God-given spiritual gifts. We are one body with many members, and each member has a specific place and a special spiritual endowment that benefits the body. There are no unimportant or unneeded members of the body of Christ. Every member has value and plays a vital part in the body functioning as a single spiritual unit. The Holy Spirit is the one who distributes the gifts to the members of the body. We don't get to select the gift of our own choosing. Our spiritual gifts are chosen for us and distributed to us by the Holy Spirit. Not only that, but the Holy Spirit also empowers us in the exercising of the gifts. We have no reason to become jealous of others as they use what God has given to them. And we have no reason to think less of anyone because they aren't involved in what we are passionate about. We are responsible and accountable for what God has graciously given to us. God uses us as we use what He has given us for His use. So we get in where we fit in, and as the body is edified, God is glorified.

I am a noisy gong or a clanging cymbal...I am
nothing...I gain nothing, (1 Cor. 13:1–3)

The greatest commandment is that we love God with
our entire being and our neighbor as ourselves. Jesus also gave
the commandment to love one another just as He loved us. By
this all people will know that we are His disciples, if we have
love for one another. (John 13:34-35) Love was the missing
element in the gifted Corinthian congregation. Giftedness and
sound biblical teaching, absent the love of God, amounts to
movement without forward motion. If we have been endowed
with the gift of speaking in languages that are unknown to us,
but don't have love for those to whom we are speaking, we
are noisy gongs and clanging cymbals. If we are gifted with
understanding, knowledge, great faith, and the ability to speak
under the inspiration of the Holy Spirit, and have no love, we
are nothing. If we give sacrificially of ourselves and our sub-
stance and have not love, we gain nothing. The apostle John
says, "Whoever does not love abides in death. We know that
we have passed out of death into life, because we love the
brothers and sisters" (1 John 3:14). To be gifted and loving,
what a dynamic duo!

Let all things be done for building up. (1 Cor. 14:26)

As the apostle continues to give instructions concerning the use of spiritual gifts, he admonishes the gifted Corinthian congregation to exercise their gifts for the purpose of edification. To edify is to build up. It is the act of building as a process for the purpose of spiritual benefit and advancement. When the church gathers for worship, whatever is said and done should be for the purpose of spiritually building up one another. The place of worship is often called an edifice, a building that was built up to provide a place for the building up of worshipers. When the church meets for worship and gifts are exercised, the saints should be edified. The church does not meet for the purpose of building up the egos of individuals and ministries. This is why order must be kept in the public worship service. Sometimes the voice we hear in our head is our own and not that of the Holy Spirit. Worshipers are sometimes controlled by emotions rather than by the influence of the Holy Spirit, and the end result is exhibition instead of edification. All of us are Christians under construction. We are living stones being built up as a spiritual house, with Christ as the chief cornerstone. The church is a body with Christ as the head; the church is a building with Christ as Architect and Builder. It's a privilege to be a part of His construction crew.

Now I would remind you, brothers, of the gospel
I preached to you, which you received, in which
you stand, and by which you are being saved .(1
Cor. 15:1–2)

Even though we hate to admit it, we have to be reminded of things from time to time. The things we have to be reminded of are things we don't always hold fast to. It's not often we have to be reminded of the things we love and prioritize in life. It's usually the things that are lower on our list of concerns, or things that are missing from the list. The apostle Paul's main objective during his first visit to Corinth was to preach Jesus Christ and Him crucified. He wasn't concerned about using impressive speech, but he was concerned about the Holy Spirit making an impression as he declared the plain gospel message. The gospel was presented in demonstration of the Spirit and power, and they believed. The gospel is the good news of the death, burial, and resurrection of Jesus. Paul wasn't ashamed of it because it is the power of God for salvation to everyone who believes. I would remind you, brothers and sisters, of the gospel. It was preached to you, and you accepted it. Because of its God-given eternal stability and efficacy, we stand in the gospel. It is the only saving message. Just a reminder.

Be watchful, stand firm in the faith, act like men, be strong. Let all that you do be done in love. (1 Cor. 16:13–14)

In Paul's first epistle to the church at Corinth, he addressed practices in the church that needed to be corrected. He also confronted behavior in the congregation that would weaken its testimony. They had been spiritually sleepwalking, and acting like immature children. They had been soft on sin, and instead of loving one another, they were living in strife, envy, and pride. As the letter comes to a close, he leaves them with a few final exhortations. He encourages them to be watchful. This is to be awakened in a spiritual sense. It is to be spiritually alert and on your guard, keeping your spiritual eyes open. The Corinthian Christians are also encouraged to stand fast in the faith. We must hold tight to our convictions that were formed by a renewed mind through sound biblical teaching. They are told to be brave, which is to "act like men" and to be marked by maturity. The believers are to be strong and resolute, allowing nothing to move them from their convictions and their confidence in Christ. Finally, all that they do should be done in love. God loves the very people who shake their fist at Him. Keep on loving. Love God, love your Christian brothers and sisters, and love your neighbor. We love because He first loved us.

> *Indeed, we felt that we had received the sentence of death. But that was to make us rely not on ourselves but on God who raises the dead. (2 Cor. 1:9)*

When Saul of Tarsus was saved and called to the apostolic ministry, he was commanded to go into Damascus, and there he would be told what he must do. When the Lord spoke to Ananias of Damascus about Saul, He said to him, "For I will show him how many things he must suffer for My name's sake." Our Lord was a suffering Savior, and He made it clear that in the world we would have tribulation. Saul/Paul also made it clear that we must through many tribulations enter the kingdom of God. For the believer, tribulations come in all colors, shapes, sizes, and duration. To ascertain how much pain we are experiencing, doctors will ask us to describe it on a scale of one to ten, with ten being the most severe. God will sometimes allow His children to experience affliction so severe that it seems like a death sentence. We can sometimes feel as though there is no way out of affliction because seemingly all exits have been closed. But we must remember that this is a feeling, and believers function on faith, not feelings. However, feelings are real, and they should make us rely on God. Our God is in heaven; and He does whatever He pleases (Ps. 115:3). God took dust from the ground and fashioned it into a lifeless man. He then breathed into his nostrils the breath of life, and man became a living being. God can cause one to live, and He can cause one to live again. When the Lord returns, mortality (that which is subject to death) will put on immortality (that which is not subject to death). If we are trusting Him for this, we can trust Him with everything else. For we walk by faith, not by sight.

But thanks be to God, who in Christ always
leads us in triumphal procession. (2 Cor. 2:14)

The child of God should be thankful for every spiritual victory. Thanks and praises are due God because He is the one who enables and empowers us to be victorious in spiritual warfare, in ministry, and in life. As believers we must remember that whenever we experience victory, God is the reason for it. We are walking behind Christ and following Him as we share in His victory. The battle has been fought, and the victory has been won. In this verse, Paul is thinking of the Roman ceremony called the Triumph, in which a victorious general was honored with a festive ceremonial parade through the streets of Rome. This reminds me of the annual Super Bowl parade where the victorious team is celebrated and honored. The Vince Lombardi trophy is hoisted and passed around, and the MVP is recognized. Christ is our MVP, and He always leads us in victory. Thanks be to God!

*Not that we are sufficient in ourselves to claim
anything as coming from us, but our sufficiency
is from God, who has made us competent. (2
Cor. 3:5–6)*

It is a proven biblical fact that Satan often attacks the mind of the Christian believer. All of the troubles we bring upon ourselves begin with our own misguided and prideful thinking. One of the dangers of being used in service for the Lord is to give yourself too much credit. Without the enabling power of the Holy Spirit, we are not adequately equipped or competent to serve effectively in any type of ministry. Because of our personal insufficiencies and inadequacies, we dare not think of ourselves as the source of anything that has spiritual and eternal value. The apostle Paul said to the saints at Rome, "For I know that nothing good dwells in me, that is, in my flesh" (Rom. 7:18). We are not competent or adequate within ourselves, nor are we worthy to think of ourselves as "all of that" when it comes to our laboring in the Lord. Paul said to the Corinthian congregation, "For I am the least of the apostles, unworthy to be called an apostle, because I persecuted the church of God. But by the grace of God I am what I am. I worked harder than any of them, though it was not I, but the grace of God that is with me" (1 Cor. 15:9-10). When it comes to Christian ministry and all it entails, who is sufficient for these things? The answer is a resounding, "No one!" But by the grace of God, our competency and ability comes from Him and Him alone.

There is no higher or more humbling privilege than to be called and used by God.

But we have renounced disgraceful, under-handed ways. We refuse to practice cunning or to tamper with God's word. (2 Cor. 4:2)

In 2 Corinthians 2:17, the apostle Paul said, "For we are not, like so many, peddlers of God's word, but as men of sincerity, as commissioned by God, in the sight of God we speak in Christ." In the history of the early church, it is on record that the apostles devoted themselves to prayer and to the ministry of the Word (Acts 6:4). The apostles were men of sincerity who were called and commissioned by God. They were men who feared God and were fully aware of the consequences of their actions and motivations. God has always called and commissioned men to stand before men and declare His Word, and not their own. The Old Testament prophet would stand and declare, "Thus says the Lord." We must be careful in the how and why of handling God's Word. It is a disgrace how some ministers handle God's Word in underhanded ways. It is not of God when one is deceptive and dishonest in the preaching and teaching of His Word. The preacher or teacher has no right to tamper with the inspired Word of God. God does not call hucksters and peddlers to stand before His people. All of God's preachers say the same thing. They may have different ways of saying it, but they all say the same thing. Don't be fooled and mislead.

For we know that if the tent, which is our earthly home, is destroyed, we have a building from God, a house not made with hands, eternal in the heavens. (2 Cor. 5:1)

There was no comparison between Moses' tabernacle and Solomon's temple. The first was a tent; temporary, fragile, and of lesser beauty. The second was a building; permanent, structurally solid, and a magnificent sight to behold. In the same way, there is no comparison between our earthy home and our eternal house. Paul refers to the physical human body as a tent. Like a tent, the physical body is temporary, weak, and absent of any lasting beauty. Eventually the physical body will die and return to the dust from whence it came. Afterward, decay and stench will set in. But Paul refers to the resurrected, glorified body as a building from God, a house not made with hands, eternal in the heavens. The body that we will possess in heaven is not of the earthly creation. It is from God, glorified like Christ's own glorious body and fit for heaven. The body we possess here and now is mortal (subject to death) and perishable. The body we will possess in heaven is immortal (not subject to death) and imperishable.

When Christ appears we shall be like Him because we shall see Him as He is. God has given us a blessed hope and a certain future. It will be worth it all.

Do not be unequally yoked with unbelievers.
For what partnership has righteousness with
lawlessness? Or what fellowship has light with
darkness? (2 Cor. 6:14)

The apostle Paul begins this chapter with the phrase,
"Working together with Him." He later refers to himself and
others as "servants of God." Afterward, he reminds us that we
are "the temple of the living God." What point is he trying to
make, and what timeless truth is he attempting to teach us?
Paul is placing emphasis on the doctrine of separation. When
we were saved, we were "set apart" from the world unto God to
be used by Him. Of course we must live in this world until the
time of our departure. But we no longer have fellowship and
partnership with the evil world system. Paul's New Testament
teaching is rooted in the Old Testament precepts concerning
the separation of God's people from ungodly alliances. Believers
are devoted and dedicated to God. And this should be seen in
their partnerships and affiliations. Being unequally yoked does
not apply to the marriage relationship only. Believers should
refrain from all unholy alliances. Jesus did not come into the
world to be friends with the devil. He came to destroy the
works of the evil one. Some things just don't mix.

Since we have these promises, beloved, let us cleanse ourselves from every defilement of body and spirit, bringing holiness to completion in the fear of God. (2 Cor. 7:1)

Our God is known for keeping His promises. But before we rush to claim the promises of God, we must be sure we've met the conditions for them. It has been said that obedience is motivated by God's promises more than by His commandments. The Old Testament promises quoted by Paul in 6:16–18 are designed to encourage obedient action. The Corinthian believers had been called out of idolatry. But some of them were attempting to allow their Christian beliefs to coexist with idolatrous ideologies and the doctrine of the false teachers who were opposed to Paul. God becomes our Father when we accept Christ as Lord and Savior, but intimacy with Him is necessary if we are to grow in the faith. The blood of Jesus has cleansed us from all sin for salvation, but we must cleanse ourselves from religious defilement and unholy partnerships. We have a responsibility to guard our bodies and minds from anything that could possibly hinder our spiritual growth and put distance between us and God. We are not perfect, but we should strive for perfection. We are holy, positionally speaking, and should make every effort to make holiness practical in our daily living. Having a reverence and respect for God will bring us closer to the perfection we so desperately desire. Since God has given us these promises, let us meet the conditions.

For you know the grace of our Lord Jesus Christ,
that though He was rich, yet for your sake He
become poor, so that you by His poverty might
become rich. (2 Cor 8:9)

Giving is an act of grace (2 Cor. 8:6, 7, 19). It must be motivated by the grace of God in the heart of the believer. As children of God, we are recipients and beneficiaries of His amazing grace. As God has been and continues to be gracious toward us, we have the responsibility of being gracious toward others, especially those who are of the household of faith. As believers we are familiar with the grace of our Lord Jesus Christ. His grace is what saved us, sanctifies us, and sustains us. We need grace, and He always provides the necessary amount. The grace of Christ was demonstrated through the incarnation. Because He is God the Son, everything that God the Father has belongs to Him. The earth is the LORD's and the fullness thereof, the world and those who dwell therein (Ps. 24:1). This is divine universal ownership.

Even though Christ was rich, for our sakes He became poor. He clothed Himself in the form and appearance of man, lived under self-imposed restrictions, and died on a cross like a common criminal. Those of us who believe have become spiritually rich because of His voluntary impoverishment; not to mention the privilege of being joint heirs with Christ. Giving is an act of grace. As Christ our example has done, so should we eagerly and enthusiastically do the same.

> *For I know your readiness...saying that Achaia*
> *has been ready...so that you may be ready...and*
> *find that you are not ready...so that it* (your
> gift) *may be ready. (2 Cor. 9:2–5)*

As children and servants of the Most High God, we should be ready at all times for whatever the will of God requires of us. Of course God is fully aware of the state of readiness of all the saints. But every good shepherd is also aware of the readiness and unreadiness of the sheep under his care and watch. When something needs to be done, those who are ready always step up and get it done. Paul is about the business of encouraging the Corinthian saints to contribute to the gift being collected for the impoverished saints at Jerusalem. He has used the generosity of the saints at Macedonia to motivate the Corinthians to complete what they started in this endeavor of benevolence. Having an intimate knowledge of them, he knows of their eagerness and willingness to participate in this ministry. Not only are they eager to give, they have made preparations to give. We should be willing to do for others, and make preparations that we might be ready when the time comes. We should be as eager to sow as we are to reap; as eager to scatter seed as we are to gather the harvest. Give and it shall be given to you.

For it is not the one who commends himself who is approved, but the one whom the Lord commends. (2 Cor. 10:18)

There is an old saying that goes, "It's a sorry dog that won't wag its own tail." It simply means that one should feel good about themselves and talk up their own accomplishments lest they go unnoticed. Even though I have heard this many times during church services, I don't believe this behavior is appropriate for the children of God. Every time I've heard this statement made in worship, I've thought of Proverbs 27:2, which says, "Let another praise you, and not your own mouth; a stranger, and not your own lips." If we are found boasting, we should be boasting about who God is and what He's done. If we have accomplished anything in life, God should get the glory because He has made it possible. The Message Bible says, "What you say about yourself means nothing in God's work. It's what God says about you that makes the difference" (2 Cor. 10:18). We are not dogs, and we don't have tails.

*And no wonder, for even Satan disguises him-
self as an angel of light. So it is no surprise if his
servants, also, disguise themselves as servants of
righteousness. (2 Cor. 11:14–15)*

For everything that God has, Satan has a counterfeit. As a matter of fact, Satan himself is a counterfeit. This is something that the apostle Paul was gravely concerned about. In verse 28 he said, "There is the daily pressure on me of my anxiety for all the churches." As one who was called by God to be an apostle, he had a genuine concern for churches that were being influenced by false apostles. In this chapter, he refers to them as false apostles and deceitful workmen, who disguise themselves as apostles of Christ. But we shouldn't be surprised because Satan also disguises himself for the purpose of deception. Satan is an angel, but he is no angel of light. He is a fallen and disgraced angel who attempted to usurp the power and authority of God almighty. He has continued this attempt throughout the ages. He majors in stealing, killing, destroying, lying, deceiving, and causing doubt, disunity, and confusion. He is the exact opposite of what God is, yet he disguises himself as an angel of light. Satan has servants who disguise themselves as servants of righteousness. Concerning false teachers, false prophets, and false apostles, Jesus said, "You will recognize them by their fruits" (Matt. 7:20). Wolves may disguise themselves by wearing sheep's clothing, but they will always leave wolf tracks. Beware and be aware.

For children are not obligated to save up for their parents, but parents for their children. (2 Cor. 12:14)

This Scripture passage means exactly what it says. However, Paul's love and affection for the saints at Corinth causes him to see them as his own spiritual children. And like any good parent, he doesn't want to be a burden to them but a blessing. Like any devoted parent, he is not seeking what the children possess, but he is seeking the children for who and whose they are. He is concerned about his relationship with them and their spiritual wellbeing. As their spiritual father, Paul has been placed in the peculiar position of having to defend his apostleship. This should never have happened because they were fully aware of his labor of love among them. They should have been defending and commending him. His ministry wasn't inferior to anyone's, and he performed all the signs of an apostle in their midst. There was no reason for him to have to commend himself to anyone, especially to them. Dedicated parents don't have to commend themselves to their own children. They have already spent and been spent, labored and toiled, saved and sacrificed for the sake of their children. But this is what parents are obligated to do. And good parents do it out of obligation, coupled with love. Proverbs 13:22 says, "A good man leaves an inheritance to his children's children."— financial, but especially spiritual.

Examine yourselves, to see whether you are in
the faith. Test yourselves. (2 Cor. 13:5)

A little boy went into the neighborhood store and asked to use the phone. After receiving permission from the owner, he called a woman and offered to provide lawn service for her. She stated that she was completely satisfied with her present lawn service. He thanked her for her time and hung up. The store-owner overheard the conversation and told the boy that he was sorry about his not getting the woman's business. The little boy explained to the storeowner that he already had the woman's business. He then said, "I was just checking up on myself." It's good to check up on ourselves periodically. Self-examination is a way of life for the Christian who wants to grow spiritually and live according to the Word and will of God. The unexamined life is really a life that's not worth living. We must practice putting ourselves on trial; examining and cross-examining ourselves. We must take the oath, promising to tell the truth, the whole truth, and nothing but the truth. Honest self-examination, followed by confession and repentance is good for the soul. Do I have the witness of the Holy Spirit within me? Do I love the brothers and sisters? Do I love the Lord? Do I practice righteousness? Do I cheerfully and regularly give to my church? Is my church a priority in my life? Am I faithful? Am I willing to serve? These are some of the questions. Now grade your own paper.

So extremely zealous was I for the traditions of my fathers. (Gal. 1:14)

A tradition is a long-established or inherited pattern of culture, beliefs, or practices. A tradition may also be defined as a doctrine, practice, or injunction delivered or communicated from one to another, whether human or divine. This was the apostle Paul's use of tradition in the context of Gal. 1:14. Like so many others, prior to his conversion, Paul was extremely zealous for what had been handed down to him from previous generations. In every cultural setting, much has been passed from one generation to another.

Our traditions have both human and divine origins. As people seeking to please the Lord, we should be more concerned about the commandments of God than the traditions of men. Many people are ignorant of the fact that there is a cultural reason for every church tradition. And because many of these cultural situations no longer exist, there is no longer a need for many church traditions. However, there are those who would rather burn the church down than give up their traditions. This is an example of zeal without knowledge. Paul's example is a great one to follow. After meeting Jesus and experiencing the revelation of God's truth, Paul gave up "the traditions of the elders" that were contrary to the Word of God. When we have come to know the Word who became flesh, and have grown in His Word, we lay aside the traditions of men. Are we zealous for the traditions of men or the Word of God?

> *For he who worked through Peter for his apostolic ministry to the circumcised worked also through me for mine to the Gentiles. (Gal. 2:8)*

Prior to the Lord's ascension He instructed His disciples to wait for the promise of the Father, which was the Holy Spirit. They would need the Spirit's enabling power to live the Christian life and to fulfill the ministries assigned to them. The Holy Spirit would empower them to be the Lord's witnesses in Jerusalem and all Judea and Samaria, and to the end of the earth. Some of them would be witnesses in the city of Jerusalem and die there. Others would suffer persecution and death in other countries. The Holy Spirit empowered them to not only proclaim what they had seen, heard, and experienced, but He also enabled them to suffer, bleed, and die as did their Lord. A witness is literally a martyr, one who willingly suffers death rather than renounce their religion. The same Spirit who worked in and through them for their ministries is working in and through present-day believers for theirs. God empowers all of His children to fulfill their designated callings. He sends us to whomever He chooses, but the same Spirit empowers us. He empowers those who seem to be influential, and those who seem to be pillars in the church. But He shows no partiality and uses all of His children according to His plan for their life and the life of His church. How is His plan working out in your life?

Christ redeemed us from the curse of the law
by becoming a curse for us; for it is written,
"Cursed is everyone who is hanged on a tree"
(Gal. 3:13).

Salvation is by grace alone, through faith alone, in Christ alone. Not a single Old Testament saint was saved by keeping the law. Salvation has always been by grace through faith. The patriarch Abraham is often referred to as the father of the faithful. Abraham believed God, and it was counted to him as righteousness. This was an imputed righteousness. The Old Testament law contains 613 commandments and prohibitions that no one is capable of fully obeying. Failure to perfectly keep the entire law brings judgment and condemnation; a curse. If only one commandment or prohibition is violated, we are guilty of the whole and are, therefore cursed, because the law is one. But the good news is, Christ has redeemed us from the curse of the law by becoming a curse for us. When Christ was crucified on His cross, He bore our sins and became a curse for us. The suffering of Christ on the tree (cross) was the result of our sin being placed on Him and the wrath of God being poured out on Him. Because of His voluntary sacrifice, every child of God is blessed rather than cursed. When the devil reminds you of your past, remind him of his future.

*Have I then become your enemy by telling you
the truth? (Gal. 4:16)*

Human beings are fickle and temperamental, and change like the wind. They can wake up in the morning loving you as a friend and, before bedtime, hate you as an enemy. This applies not only to the people of the world, but to the people in the church as well. It's amazing how biblical truth can be proclaimed to people, and readily and enthusiastically received by them until they hear some so-called "new" truth. Now they accept the proclaimer of the so-called "new" truth and separate themselves from the message and messenger of unadulterated biblical truth. Every God-called and doctrinally sound pastor has had the experience of seeing people under his care defect to some ear-tickling deceiver. We should always beware of those who establish and build their ministries by tearing down the ministries of others. I would also advise that we be leery of those who dare to criticize and condemn the very thing God has used to bring us along on our spiritual journey. Unadulterated biblical truth is hard to come by, and it has always been this way. Most people aren't interested in the rightly divided word of truth. People prefer religious entertainment, dynamic personalities, and the attractions of the worldly. Jesus said, "If you abide in My word, you are truly My disciples, and you will know the truth, and the truth will set you free" (John 8:31-32). We should love biblical truth and those who proclaim it.

"the one who is troubling you" . . ."those who unsettle you" (Gal. 5:10, 12).

Legalism is the doctrine that salvation is gained through the strict adherence to certain rules and regulations. Legalism had crept into the churches in the region of Galatia, and the apostle Paul wrote to them that it might be rooted out. False teachers were troubling and confusing them by requiring add-ons to faith in order to be saved. This was not the same gospel that Paul had preached to them. Paul assured them that the truth would prevail, and the false teachers who were confusing them would be judged by God. Paul also wished that those who were disturbing and unsettling them would be unable to attract more followers. Salvation is by grace through faith in our Lord and Savior Jesus Christ. There are no add-ons! Stand on this truth, and don't allow anyone to trouble or unsettle you.

Keep watch on yourself, lest you too be tempted.
(Gal. 6:1)

Life in the fellowship of believers involves correcting and restoring those who have gone astray. However, if we dare to correct others, we must keep careful watch over our own lives. We are often quick to judge and condemn others for the very sins that we commit. This is what Jesus was referring to in John 8 when He said, "Let him who is without sin among you be the first to throw a stone at her." All of the woman's accusers left because they were guilty of the same sin. Charles Spurgeon would lecture to his ministerial students about "The Minister's Self Watch." I would suggest that we lecture to ourselves about "The Christian's Self Watch." The prophet Jeremiah said, "The heart is deceitful above all things, and desperately sick; who can understand it" (Jer. 17:9)? We should be careful about saying what we would never do and what we would never do again. All of us have done things we said we would never do, and all of us have done things we said we would never do again. As a child of God, there are things we will never do, and there are things we will never do again. But we must remember that the potential is still there. As children of God, we must give attention to ourselves because we will be tested, tried, and tempted. When temptation comes, God will provide a way of escape, but we must choose to take it.

The immeasurable greatness of His power
toward us who believe (Eph. 1:19)

Jesus encourages us to always pray. Paul encourages us to pray without ceasing. James assures us of the result of fervent prayer. I believe that one of the reasons we should always pray, and pray without ceasing, is because there is so much for us to pray about. Paul gave thanks to God for the saints at Ephesus. He did not cease to pray for them, and he remembered them in his prayers. One of his prayer requests for them was that they might know what is the immeasurable greatness of God's power toward us who believe. God is the only omnipotent being. He has all power. His power and the greatness of it cannot be measured. Political power can and must be measured. Economic power can be measured. The power of human influence can be measured. There is a limit to the power that God allows man to possess; it can be measured. We ought to ponder the immeasurable greatness of God's power toward us who believe. The demonstration of the immeasurable greatness of God's power is the resurrection and exaltation of Christ. God raised Jesus from the dead. After His resurrection, God seated Him in the place of honor and supreme privilege, far above all rule and authority and power and dominion, and above every title given. He is over everything, not only in this age but also in the one to come. O that we might know the infinite power of almighty God.

Following the course of this world, following the
prince of the power of the air (Eph. 2:2)

Prior to our receiving salvation through God's grace, we were the walking dead. We were the walking dead because we were walking in trespasses and sin. Sin always leads to death. And if we were walking in sin, we were also walking in death. We were the walking dead. Our walk is our way of living and passing our lives; our lifestyle. Ours was a lifestyle of death and separation from God because this is how we were walking. And we can be sure that our lives are styled by the one that we are following.

Whether we realize it or not, we are all following someone or something. At that time we were following the course of this world. We were going with the flow of the world system which doesn't value or believe the Word of God. Without being aware of it (sometimes), we were following the "god of this world" and the "prince of the power of the air" who leads this world system. We were following the one who, by demonic influence, has always attempted to usurp the authority over our lives that only God possesses. But because of the richness of God's mercy and His great love for us, He made us alive together with Christ. We were dead; now we are alive. God has already raised us from spiritual death to newness of life. Now with hopeful anticipation, we eagerly await eternal life in the glorious presence of God.

Now to Him who is able to do far more abun-
dantly than all that we ask or think, according
to the power at work in us. (Eph. 3:20)

We know that our God is able. We know from reading the holy Scriptures that our God is able to create and recreate. He is able to heal and make whole. God is able to save and deliver. He is able to open what no man can close and close what no man can open. God is able to shut the mouths of lions and calm stormy seas. He is able to comfort us in all of our affliction and give rest to our weary souls. He can lift up bowed down heads and bring peace to troubled minds. You get the picture; our God is able. We also know that God is able from the experience of answered prayer. All of us have gone to God in prayer, asking, seeking, and knocking. As a result, He has given; we have found; and it has been opened to us. What we know of God's ability from Scripture is based on our reading and thinking. What we know of God's ability from experience is based on answered prayer and witnessing His mighty works in and around us and in the lives of others. But there is so much more to God's ability than what we have read and experienced. God is able to do things that are beyond our human comprehension and imagination.

He is familiar with all our ways, but His ways are past finding out. What a mighty God we serve.

Let no corrupting talk come out of your mouths,
but only such as is good for building up, as fits
the occasion, that it may give grace to those who
hear. (Eph. 4:29)

King David prayed on one occasion, "Let the words of my mouth and the meditation of my heart be acceptable in your sight, O Lord, my rock and my redeemer" (Ps. 19:14). The ponderings of the heart will determine the words that come from the mouth. As children of the Most High God, our speech matters to Him, and it should matter to us. As born-again believers, we should always use our best language, whether spoken or written. This includes our social media posts. The Christian Standard Bible says, "No foul language should come from your mouth." The word for "corrupting" refers to that which is rotten, putrid, and foul, such as spoiled fruit and rotten meat. The sight and stench is very unpleasant and difficult to endure. It is never appropriate for professing Christians to use foul language. We are to be about the business of building up people in a godly and spiritual manner. Jesus and the apostles used seemingly harsh language at times but never foul or profane. We are to speak the truth in love for the purpose of edification. Our speech should always be gracious, seasoned with salt. Watch your mouth.

Try to discern what is pleasing to the Lord.
Understand what the will of the Lord is.
(Eph. 5:10, 17)

Two of the most important things in life are discerning what is pleasing to the Lord and understanding what the will of the Lord is. Here we have before us discernment and understanding. We are also faced with the responsibility of pleasing the Lord and knowing His will. It all begins with the new birth, that is, being born again, having new life in Christ Jesus. This is first and foremost because the natural (unconverted) person does not accept the things of the Spirit of God, for they are folly to him, and he is not able to understand them because they are spiritually discerned. (1 Cor. 2:14) Believers are constantly testing, proving, and distinguishing what is pleasing and acceptable to the Lord. We also search the Scriptures to discover for ourselves what He deems acceptable and pleasing. By practicing spiritual discernment and exposing ourselves to the Word of God, it becomes clear to us what is acceptable to Him. It is also necessary that we understand what His will is. What is God's disposition toward His children, His church, and His world? What about racism, injustice, oppression, and every other societal ill? The Word of God and the Spirit of God can answer these questions and solve these problems. Discern and understand.

An ambassador in chains (Eph. 6:20)

An ambassador is an authorized messenger or representative. American ambassadors are representatives to other countries where they serve to promote American interests. Ambassadors of the United States enjoy many perks and benefits. They have paid staff, free housing, bodyguards, and an automobile and driver. They can enjoy the rich culture of the countries where they serve. Their salaries are commensurate with their education and experience, and they enjoy free housing and an expense account. Other benefits include federal health care and retirement plans. Additionally, diplomatic immunity protects the ambassador from an inadvertent legal slip or blunder. As an ambassador for Christ, Paul did not enjoy any of these perks. We know he had no diplomatic immunity because he wrote from prison in Rome. He was an ambassador in chains. He considered himself as the "prisoner of the Lord." Even as an ambassador in chains, for him, the mission had not changed. His ministry was still the ministry of reconciliation. Paul requested the prayers of the Ephesian believers. He didn't request prayer to be released from prison or for his life to be made easier. His request was for words to be given to him that he might boldly proclaim the gospel of Jesus Christ. As believers, we are ambassadors for Christ, with or without chains, and with or without a thorn. The message from our Master is, "Be reconciled to God."

I thank my God in all my remembrance of you.
(Phil. 1:3)

The apostle Paul had fond memories of his ministry among the saints at Philippi. As he looks back on his experiences with them, he gives thanks and praises to God for them. What a blessed relationship he obviously had with them. Whenever Paul prayed for them, his petitions were accompanied by thanksgiving and joy. They had demonstrated consistency in their partnership in the gospel of Jesus Christ. It appears as though he was able to serve among them with joy, and not with grief. How many people have we labored with in the Lord's vineyard whose partnership moves us to thank and praise God for them? It's a blessing from God to be able to remember people with fondness and gratefulness. God blesses us to be a blessing. We should seek to make our relationships with others pleasant, and drama and stress free. Our interaction with people should be in a spirit that makes them glad to see us coming, and sad to see us going. Let's live among people in a manner that causes them to thank God for us as they remember us. Will we be missed when we're gone?

Do nothing from rivalry or conceit, but in humility count others more significant than yourselves. (Phil. 2:3)

An exhortation such as this would be widely frowned upon in today's world, where aggressiveness, self-importance, and pride are in our DNA. As born-again believers, it is not God's will that we become rivals or competitors. We are all servants laboring in different parts of the same vineyard, serving the same Master. Paul encourages us to be like-minded, having the same love, being in full accord, and of one mind. He is emphasizing unity through humility. A few days ago, I participated in a team event. We were one team that consisted of four people. We all had the same goal in mind. There was discussion but no arguing. Every decision was made for the benefit of the team, not the individual team member. We all made up for each other's mistakes and shortcomings. The efforts of each individual contributed to the success of the team. We started as a team and finished as a team. And I might add that we were able to enjoy shared success as the result of our unity through humility. What we do matters, and our motives matter just as much. We often say, "It's not about us; it's about the Lord." If we really feel this way, then let us lay aside selfish ambition and personal glory, and labor on behalf of the team. We should look inward and ask ourselves, "If every team member was just like me, what kind of team would our team be?"

*And glory in Christ Jesus and put no confidence
in the flesh. (Phil. 3:3)*

Jesus Christ our Lord is the only person we should ever
boast about. He is the eternal Word who dwelt in the bosom
of the Father in eternity past. He was miraculously conceived
and born of the virgin Mary. He was the perfect child who
submitted Himself to the parenting of Joseph and Mary. As a
boy, He grew in wisdom and in stature and in favor with God
and man. He submitted Himself to the baptism of John, even
though He had no sin to repent of or to be cleansed from. He
did only what the Father told Him to do and spoke only what
the Father told Him to speak. He went about doing good while
performing miracles of mercy. No one could speak the way He
spoke, and no one could do the works that He did. Eventually
He offered Himself as the perfect sacrifice for the sin of the
world. He died on an old rugged cross while asking His Father
to forgive His executioners. He was buried, but on the third
day God raised Him from the dead. All authority in heaven
and earth was given to Him along with the name that is above
every name. For these reasons, all of our boasting should be
in Him. We should have enough sanctified common sense to
know that in our flesh dwells no good thing. Therefore, we put
no confidence in our flesh, but we make our boast in and about
our Lord and Savior Jesus Christ.

For I have learned in whatever situation I am
to be content. (Phil. 4:11)

It is a well-known biblical fact that God blesses us through people. This is one of the reasons He brings people together, that they might be a blessing to one another. Paul had been a blessing to the church at Philippi, and they had been a blessing to him as well. In this passage, he was expressing his appreciation for all they had done for him. He was grateful and used this time to teach a lesson on contentment. We can't teach what we haven't learned. Paul had to learn contentment. He learned that contentment is satisfaction found in Christ. He learned that our sufficiency is in Christ. Lessons learned must also be lived. Therefore, he lived contentment. He wrote from prison, but he was content. He had suffered the loss of all things, but he was content. Contentment is needed when one has little; contentment is needed when one has much. It is needed in whatever state you find yourself in. Paul learned and lived contentment because he was connected to Christ. Contentment comes after the soul has been anchored in the Lord.

Making peace by the blood of His cross
(Col. 1:20)

In our former unredeemed life we did not know and had never experienced genuine peace. We were familiar with peace from a secular perspective. We understood peace between nations and other factions. We were aware of peace treaties between adversaries to end hostilities and abstain from further fighting. All of us were aware of people or groups who enjoyed being in a state of mutual harmony. There is also the freedom of the mind from annoyance, distraction, and anxiety, a state of tranquility and serenity. And certainly, we were familiar with peace in personal relationships. But there is another kind of peace that is other-worldly. This peace is not of this world but came into the world through the Prince of Peace. Jesus said, "Peace I leave with you; My peace I give to you. Not as the world gives do I give to you. Let not your hearts be troubled, neither let them be afraid" (John 14:27). Now that we have been justified by faith, we have peace with God through our Lord Jesus Christ. Prior to salvation, we did not have peace with God. We were children of wrath, following the prince of the power of the air (Satan), rather than the Prince of Peace. But Jesus made peace for us by the blood of His cross. When He was on the cross, we were on His mind. The only genuine and eternal peace is that which comes from Christ. No Jesus, no peace; know Jesus, know peace.

Abounding in thanksgiving (Col. 2:7)

Christians should be the most thankful people in the world. When we seriously ponder what God has done for us through Christ, we should abound in thanksgiving. As we consider the bountiful blessings bestowed upon us, our hearts should overflow with gratefulness. God always treats us better than we deserve; and we should be thankful. He awakens us each day with mercy and puts us to bed each night with grace, and we should be thankful. We should abound in thanksgiving because our sin debt has been paid. All of us were spiritual debtors. A record of debt is kept on everyone.

Everyone is chargeable and liable. And everyone is also delinquent. But Jesus vouched for us; He posted our bail, He paid our ransom, and He redeemed us. He took our IOUs and nailed them to His cross, cancelling our debt. This is what He did for every believer. And our hearts should be overflowing with thanksgiving. People often ask the Lord to fill their cups and let them overflow. What He has already done is enough to fill our hearts, causing them to overflow with thanksgiving.

Christ who is your life (Col. 3:4)

Eternal life is not only life without end, it is also a higher kind of life. It is a higher kind of life because we have been raised with Christ. Now that we are experiencing and enjoying this higher kind of life, we are inclined to seek the things that are above, where Christ is seated at the right hand of God. Eternal life involves a renewing of the mind; therefore, we are to set our minds on things that are above, not on things that are on the earth. This gift of eternal life is in Christ. He is in us, and we are in Him. If anyone is in Christ, he is a new creation. The old has passed away, and the new has come. To the Christian, Christ is the most important thing in life. As a matter of fact, to the Christian, Christ is our life. We often say, "Sports is his life. Music is his life. Fishing and hunting is his life. Shopping is her life. Hearing and spreading gossip is their life." But for the born-again believer, Christ is our life. Jesus said, "I came that they may have life and have it abundantly" (John 10:10). Jesus didn't come to offer us what we already had. Prior to salvation, we were not living; we were simply existing. We began to live at the moment of our conversion. The apostle Paul said to the Philippians, "For to me to live is Christ" (Phil. 1:21). He said to the Galatians, "It is no longer I who live, but Christ who lives in me. And the life I now live in the flesh I live by faith in the Son of God, who loved me and gave Himself for me" (Gal. 2:20). When Christ who is your life appears, then you also will appear with Him in glory. Let the church say *Amen*!

Tychicus, beloved brother, faithful minister and fellow servant (Col. 4:7)

The Lord's churches would benefit greatly from having more men like Tychicus. His name means "fortunate." Fortunate means coming or happening by good luck; bringing a benefit or good that was not expected or was not foreseen as certain; and receiving some unexpected good. Included in one of the definitions of fortunate is the word *luck*. The word luck is not a part of the Christian vocabulary. As believers we don't believe in luck, good or bad. We don't believe in chance or happenstance. But we do believe in the sovereignty and providence of God. Tychicus was fortunate indeed to be saved by the grace of God. Salvation came to him and us by the sovereignty and providence of God. Like Tychicus, we are fortunate to experience salvation and all of its benefits, which we did not foresee or expect. We are fortunate to have received God's grace and God's gifts. Because of what God has given and equipped us with, our churches are fortunate to have us. But this is true only if we can be described as faithful fellow servants. Tychicus was considered a beloved brother because of the faithful service he rendered to the Lord and His churches. We love all of our brothers and sisters in Christ. But a beloved brother or sister in the church is one who can be counted on to render faithful service. Their works speak for them.

And you became imitators of us and of the Lord.
(1 Thess. 1:6)

In his epistle to the church at Thessalonica, Paul does not thank the Thessalonian converts for their response to the gospel. Instead, he thanks God for their response to the gospel message. The reason for this is because Paul did not consider coming to faith in Christ as a matter of human initiative or achievement, but of God's initiative and call. God always initiates salvation. Salvation is always a matter of God's choice and call. Whenever salvation occurs, it is the result of God at work in the preaching of the gospel, and in the heart of the hearer who responds to the gospel message. Paul said, "You became imitators (followers) of us and of the Lord." He says to the church at Corinth, "I urge you then, be imitators of me" (1 Cor. 4:16). He also says to the church at Corinth, "Be imitators of me, as I am of Christ" (1 Cor. 11:1). The Thessalonian believers became imitators (followers) of Paul and the Lord, after having received (accepted, resigned themselves to) the Word of God. In order for this to happen, the Holy Spirit has to make ready the heart of the hearer. Beware of the spirit of resistance and defiance in yourselves and in others. Spirit-filled believers follow Christ and His appointed leaders, as prescribed by His Word.

And we also thank God constantly for this, that when you received the Word of God, which you heard from us, you accepted it not as the word of men but as what it really is, the Word of God. (1 Thess. 2:13)

The Bible really is the Word of God. Man would never write a book that condemns what he loves and commends what he hates. Nothing makes a preacher/pastor happier and more thankful than seeing people accept the Word of God as what it really is. Paul said to Timothy, "All Scripture is breathed out by God and profitable for teaching, for reproof, for correction, and for training in righteousness" (2 Tim. 3:16). Paul was constantly thanking God for the Thessalonians' reception and acceptance of the Word of God as the Word of God. In order for one to grow and mature in the Lord, he must have a high view of the Scriptures. We are not over the Word of God to handle it as we please. The church and the individual believer are under the authority of the Word. The Word of God is over us. We have no right to dismiss or disobey it. It should be hidden (treasured) in our hearts that we might not sin against God. And if (when) we sin, we have an Advocate with the Father, Jesus Christ the righteous, who is the eternal Word. Jesus said, "Man shall not live by bread alone, but by every word that comes from the mouth of God" (Matt. 4:4).

For you yourselves know that we are destined for this. (1 Thess. 3:3)

There are three kinds of suffering. Common suffering is what all mankind must endure simply because we live in a fallen world cursed by sin. Carnal suffering is the kind we bring on ourselves as a consequence of personal sin. Be not deceived: God is not mocked, for whatever one sows, that will he also reap. (Gal. 6:7)

Christian suffering is what believers must endure simply because they are children of God. This is suffering for Jesus's sake. When it comes to Christian suffering, we must understand that all of our afflictions and tribulations are appointed by God. This is what the apostle Paul is reminding the saints at Thessalonica. Concerning his afflictions and theirs, he says, "For you yourselves know that we are destined for this." Every believer is subject to the sufferings, afflictions, and tribulations that have been divinely set and appointed for them. Consider the fact that our Savior was a suffering Savior. All of His suffering was appointed by God. A disciple is not above his teacher, nor a servant above his master. But suffering is not how or where it all ends. For the joy that was set before Him, Jesus endured the cross, despising the shame, and is seated at the right hand of the throne of God. (Heb. 12:2) If we suffer with Him we will also reign with Him. The trials and the triumphs are divinely appointed by God. You yourselves know this.

Do so more and more. Do this more and more.
(1 Thess. 4:1, 10)

When the Thessalonians were converted to Christianity they were instructed in how they ought to live and to please God. And even as the apostle Paul wrote this epistle to them, they were actually doing what they were taught. They were hearers and doers of the Word. James said, "So whoever knows the right thing to do and fails to do it, for him it is sin" (James 4:17). For them, sins of omission were just as egregious as sins of commission. They were presently living as they should and seeking to please God. But Paul asked and urged them to do so more and more. On the subject of brotherly love, they really didn't need anyone to write to them, because they were taught by God to love one another. And loving one another is exactly what they were presently doing. They understood the command to love God with your entire being, and your neighbor as yourself. These saints knew that outsiders would identify them as disciples of Christ by the love that they had for one another. But Paul urged them to do this more and more. As we grow in the Lord and become more intimate with Him, we begin to live for Him and please Him more and more. This kind of spiritual growth also enables us to love one another more and more. Spiritual growth and intimacy with God always lead us to more and more.

Be patient with them all .(1 Thess. 5:14)

We have always heard that patience is a virtue. We have all had to wait patiently for God to answer our prayers. We have waited patiently for situations and circumstances to get better. We have discovered that patience is sometimes needed in every area of our lives. Even now we are patiently waiting for the Lord's return. But how is our patience with people? Particularly speaking, how is our patience with people who are not where we are (or where we pretend to be) spiritually? Paul instructs the Thessalonians to be at peace among themselves. This requires patience. He urges them to admonish (warn) the idle; those who are unruly and disorderly. This really requires patience, and you may eventually be forced to go through the process of church discipline. He urges them to encourage the fainthearted. It takes much patience, comfort, and the grace of God to encourage the discouraged. The apostle wants them to help the weak. My mother would often say, "We know where we've been, but we don't know where we're going. And we don't know who will have to help us one day." We may be strong today, but tomorrow could be another story. We who are strong have an obligation to bear with the failings of the weak and not to please ourselves. Since God is patient with all, we should be patient as well.

> *Therefore we ourselves boast about you in the*
> *churches of God. (2 Thess. 1:4)*

The people of God should always talk the church up rather than putting it down. Even though the people of the world put the church down, even they will occasionally speak well of it. What people of the world occasionally do, we should do consistently. We are not to boast about ourselves, but it's good to boast about others. Remember, Proverbs 27:2 says, "Let another praise you, and not your own mouth; a stranger, and not your own lips." It is a blessing from God to have church members that we can boast about. And we ought to thank God for them because it's really not them but the grace of God that's with them. Salvation is by grace, and so are all the things that accompany salvation. When the saints are growing in their faith, we should talk them up and give God thanks. When their love for one another is increasing, we should talk them up and give thanks to God. When they are being steadfast in the faith, we should talk them up and give thanks to God. When they are walking by faith and not by sight, especially in the midst of persecutions and afflictions, we should talk them up and give thanks to God. As we talk them up and give thanks to God for them, we pray that God would send more believers who are like them.

These are the ones who get ministry done.

*Therefore, God sends them a strong delu-
sion, so that they may believe what is false. (2
Thess. 2:11)*

The truth is sometimes like strong medicine, hard to swallow and hard to stomach. But if we take it, it will surely cure what ails us. Some people will deny their sickness in order to avoid the prescribed remedy. But the sickness remains, and their health continues to get worse. Others will deny sickness because of their self-perceived invincibility. They don't consider themselves to be like everyone else. They believe that there's no way they could possibly be in need of healing. Therefore they deceive themselves, refuse treatment, and eventually die from their disorder. All of these scenarios are common as it relates to the spiritual health of prideful human beings. The pride in man convinces him that he is spiritually whole. This is believing what is false. The unsaved believe lies rather than truth and prefer darkness rather than light. They call good evil and call evil good. These will ask for Barabbas, and call for the crucifixion of Christ.

People with a mindset bent toward wickedness are already deceived, and God will continue to give them up to more wickedness, and will eventually give them over to a reprobate (debased) mind. In His omniscience (all-knowingness) He is fully aware of he who refuses to acknowledge Him and glorify Him as God. To them, He gives enough rope for them to hang themselves. This is the result of strong delusion. Do not be deceived. Jesus is the Way, the Truth, and the Life.

And that we may be delivered from wicked and
evil men (2 Thess. 3:2)

The apostle Paul had a habit of praying for, remembering, and thanking God for believers who came to faith through his preaching. He possessed a genuine concern for them, and they were always in his heart, thoughts, and prayers. But he would sometimes request of them prayers on his own behalf. He constantly prayed for them, and he didn't mind asking them to pray for him. It is also noted that he was always specific in his requests for prayer. Here, Paul specifically requests prayer that the Word of the Lord might spread rapidly and be honored by those who will hear it. He also requested prayer for deliverance from wicked and evil men. As the Word of the Lord was being preached, it began to spread. And as the Word of the Lord spread, wicked and evil men spread out as they intensified their opposition to its message and its messengers. Even as Paul requested prayer of them concerning wicked and evil men, he reminds them that the Lord is faithful, and will guard them against the evil one. When wicked and evil men aggressively oppose the gospel message and its messengers, they are being used by the evil one (Satan). But we can pray. We all need prayer.

But I received mercy for this reason, that in me, as the foremost, Jesus Christ might display His perfect patience as an example to those who were to believe in Him for eternal life. (1 Tim. 1:16)

The apostle Paul is known for having an attitude of gratitude. He never forgot where he came from, and he never got over the fact that God saved him. He was grateful to God for choosing him to serve as an apostle. He was thankful to God for entrusting him with the gospel, and for enabling him to fulfill his calling. One of the reasons Paul was so thankful is because of his past life. Prior to being saved, he was a blasphemer. He was abusive toward the church and vehemently spoke evil of it and Christ. As a persecutor of the church, like a bloodhound, he pursued it and committed acts of violence against it. Like Paul, it's important that we remember from whence we've come. It keeps us from becoming proud. It keeps our gratitude alive. It makes us want to do better. And it is an encouragement to others. Paul saw himself as the foremost sinner; sinner number one. But God used him to demonstrate His amazing grace and His marvelous mercy toward even the worst of sinners. God transforms our lives in such wonderful ways that others see the changes and are sometimes inspired to answer the call to follow Jesus.

*Who desires all people to be saved and to come
to the knowledge of the truth. (1 Tim. 2:4)*

The apostle Peter said that the Lord is "not wishing that
any should perish, but that all should reach repentance" (2 Pet.
3:9). The apostle Paul said about God that He "desires all people
to be saved and to come to the knowledge of the truth." The
Bible is emphatically clear about God's desire for all people
to be saved.

However, a desire is not necessarily an expectation. One
of the things we humans have in common with the divine is
the experience of unfulfilled desires. Because God is omniscient (all-knowing), He doesn't have any unmet expectations.
Because of this, unlike us humans, God doesn't experience dis-
appointment. He already knows what will and won't happen
in this world. But all of the things He desires to happen won't
take place. Whatever God decrees to happen will come to pass.
Yet His will isn't always done. God knew before the foundation
of the world who would be saved. But we don't possess this
knowledge. Therefore we are instructed to pray for all people.
All means *all*. Because of the finiteness of our human understanding and our periodic hardness of heart, we write certain
people off and stop praying for them. Instead of doing this, let
us pray: Your kingdom come, Your will be done, on earth as
it is in heaven.

The church of the living God, the pillar and foundation of truth (1 Tim. 3:15)

The church is the only entity on earth that God attaches His name to. To be clear, the church is the called out assembly of saints who have trusted Jesus Christ for salvation. He is the Founder and Head of the church, as well as the Author and Finisher of our faith. The true church is about truth. That is, divine truth, gospel truth, reality as opposed to falsehood, fables, and fiction. There is one true and living God who is the Creator of all things, and the church came out of Him. Jesus Christ is the truth. He is the eternal Word of God; truth incarnate, and the teacher of divine truth. The Holy Spirit is the Spirit of truth, one who reveals divine truth and enables us to wise up to the Word of truth. Christians are those who know and believe the truth, and are followers of Christ, the true vine. Again, the church is about truth. The church is known as the pillar and foundation of truth. A pillar, or column, is something that stands by itself or supports a building. The church is a pillar that upholds the truth of God's Word. Truth—learn it, love it, and live it.

Until I come, devote yourself to the public reading of Scripture, to exhortation, to teaching. (1 Tim. 4:13)

Paul writes to Timothy to encourage him in the ministry. Paul knows that Timothy is busy with his pastoral duties, but he doesn't want him to neglect three things of significance: reading, exhortation, and teaching. The apostle wants Timothy to make sure that the Word of God is consistently read in the public worship setting, which is vitally important because so many people fail to read it privately. According to *USA Today*, 11 percent of Americans read the Bible daily, and over half read it once per month or not at all. According to the Barna Research Group, 18 percent of those claiming to be saved read it daily, and 23 percent of those claiming to be saved never read it. But we should be devoted to reading the Bible publicly and privately. It is the Word of God with God as its author. It is our first and final word about God, Jesus, the Holy Spirit, the church, salvation, heaven and hell, and life in general. It is able to make us wise for salvation. It is a lamp to our feet and a light to our path. It will help guide us so we won't sin against God. It will correct us when we're wrong, direct us when we are lost, and encourage us when are discouraged. God's Word will stand forever. Therefore, we should be devoted to reading it.

Do not rebuke an older man but encourage him as you would a father. Treat younger men like brothers, older women like mothers, younger women like sisters, in all purity. (1 Tim. 5:1–2)

This Spirit-inspired instruction was given by an older minister to a younger minister; a father in the ministry to his son in the ministry. There is something here that can help all of us. Christianity is a relationship with Christ and those who are Christ's. For those who would follow Christ, it's not about religion; it's about relationships. We are family. Pastor Timothy was to examine himself concerning the state of his relationships with the members of the Ephesian congregation. Every local congregation is a family within the household of faith. Like Pastor Timothy, we should love and respect each member of the congregation, and it should be evident in our interactions with them. Encourage the older men with the love and respect that you would a father. The younger men are our brothers. Let's brother our brothers with brotherly love and respect. The more mature women are our mothers. These seasoned senior sisters deserve the utmost love and respect from all of us. As members of the household of faith, we are to treat the younger women in the same manner in which we treat our own sisters. It should be one of purity. The appropriate amount of love and respect for each member of the family strengthens and sustains it, especially during times of difficulty. With love and respect mixed with the grace God, the family will be all right.

But as for you, O man of God, flee these things. Pursue righteousness, godliness, faith, love, steadfastness, gentleness. (1 Tim. 6:11)

For the child of God, there are people and things that should be avoided at all costs, especially for the pastor/preacher. Doctrine that is contrary to the words of our Lord Jesus Christ should be avoided and called out for what it is. False teachers who are full of themselves and prove by their teaching that they understand nothing should be shunned. These are the ones who make it up as they go along. Those, who, like the prosperity preachers, teach that godliness is a means of gain are depraved in mind and deprived of the truth. Stay away from them. But there is great gain in godliness with contentment. The love of money and the desire for material prosperity is the cause of all kinds of evil and the downfall of many people. This is what has caused many to stray away from the faith that was once for all delivered to the saints. But we have been commanded to flee these things, and to seek the things that are worthy of our pursuit. Righteousness, godliness, faith, love, steadfastness, and gentleness are all worthy pursuits. Go after them!

I am reminded of your sincere faith, a faith that dwelt first in your grandmother Lois and your mother Eunice and now, I am sure, dwells in you as well. (2 Tim. 1:5)

Oftentimes a special relationship exists between a father in the ministry and his son or sons. Such was the relationship between Paul and Timothy. I would also add that every Timothy needs a Paul, and every Paul needs a Timothy. Both can benefit from this type of spiritual/personal, and mentor/mentee relationship. Timothy was a young man who was well spoken of by the church in Lystra and Iconium. As a result, he became a companion and spiritual son of Paul. Now even though Timothy had a biological father who happened to be Greek, his faith was something that dwelt first in his grandmother and mother. I believe that a man should leave a spiritual inheritance to his children. However, we know that this is not always the case. The spiritual legacy that was left to Timothy was bequeathed to him by Grandmother Lois and Mother Eunice. These were women of sincere faith, and their God became Timothy's God.

Because of Paul's relationship with Timothy, he was certain of the genuineness of his faith as well. Lois means "agreeable." Eunice means "good victory." Timothy means "honoring God." The influence of these two women played a major part in the God-honoring life of Pastor Timothy.

And what you have heard from me in the presence of many witnesses entrust to faithful men who will be able to teach others also. (2 Tim. 2:2)

The apostle Paul encouraged the succession of sound biblical teaching. The Old Testament was complete at this time, and the New Testament was partially completed. God was continuing to breathe out His revelation, and holy men of God wrote as they were moved by the Holy Spirit. Pastor Timothy had known the sacred writings of the Old Testament from his youth and knew that they were able to make one wise for salvation in Christ Jesus. He had been exposed to sound biblical teaching in the synagogue and from the lips of his mother and grandmother. And he was eventually exposed to Paul's teaching, bringing it all together. Now as a pastor, he is encouraged to pass along what he and many others had learned from Paul. He now had the responsibility of entrusting to faithful men what had been entrusted to him. His task was to teach faithful men, thereby equipping them to teach others. God gives pastor-teachers, or teaching pastors to His churches. The pastor is "the teacher" in the local church. He is the resident theologian. Of course, there are other teachers in the congregation, and they should be faithful individuals who have sat and continue to sit under the pastor's teaching. Good teachers continue to learn because the more they learn, the more they realize how much they don't know. With all of the error and heresy being taught, we need a succession of sound biblical teaching.

> *But understand this, that in the last days there*
> *will come times of difficulty. For people will be*
> *lovers of self. (2 Tim. 3:1–2)*

We are living in a moment in time when people are narcissistic, selfish, and self-centered. The love that fills the average heart is a love for self rather than a love for God and others. This is a sign of the times in which we are living. We are living in the last days, which is the period of time between Christ's ascension and His return. People who are narcissistic, selfish, and self-centered always make life difficult for others. Whenever self-love is taken to the extreme, you can be sure that terrible times are coming. This problem is not only in the world, it also exists within the household of faith. As one's love shifts from God to self, one's priorities also shift. This was the problem with the church at Ephesus during the time of John's writing to the seven churches of Asia Minor. They had abandoned the love that they had at first. As a result, they were commanded to remember from where they had fallen. They were to repent and do the works they did at first. Where there is a lack of love for God, His church, and others, difficult times begin to set in. What the world needs now is love. What the church needs now is love. Love does not bring times of difficulty.

For the time is coming when people will not endure sound teaching, but having itching ears they will accumulate for themselves teachers to suit their own passions. (2 Tim. 4:3)

I stated in an earlier devotional that man would never write a book that condemns what he loves and commends what he hates. The Bible is that kind of book. The person who is not serious about the Bible is not serious about Christianity. Many professing Christians would love to divorce the Bible from Christianity. The reason for this is because they prefer looking into a "trick mirror" instead of a mirror that gives an accurate reflection of who they really are and what they really need. We are living in a time when many church people are not interested in sound (healthy) teaching. They are like children who disdain a healthy nourishing meal, but desire only what tastes good, even though it's not good for them. This is a picture of many present-day churchgoers. They attend the church that gives them what they want instead of what they need for spiritual edification and sanctification. They prefer hype over what is healthy, wholesome, and holy; religious entertainment over true worship. And it's not enough to have a teaching pastor. The question is, "What is he teaching?" The Word of God must be rightly divided; it must be cut straight. When the pastor cuts it straight, it fits into the whole of Scripture. God-called pastors and Bible teachers are not in the business of scratching itching ears. It's about the truth, the whole truth, and nothing but the truth, so help us God.

> *Therefore rebuke them sharply, that they may*
> *be sound in the faith. (Titus 1:13)*

There must always be accountability in the personal life of the believer as well as in the corporate life of the church. God has always been a God of order, and His order is clearly established in His Word. We are known to sometimes sing, "Order my steps in Your Word," and God has certainly done that. His Word, when obeyed, brings order to our personal lives and the local fellowship. Pastor Titus was commanded to put what remained into order. This is the assignment given to every pastor. No congregation has attained to the measure of the fullness of Christ. Therefore, we continue to set things in order. This may entail correcting erroneous teaching and unbiblical practices within the church. It also means ensuring that church leaders possess the biblical qualifications for leadership. Those who preach and instruct others must hold fast to sound teaching and rebuke those whose lives and lips contradict it. Teachers who refuse to follow the pattern of sound teaching must be silenced, lest they mislead and deceive the hearers. If these instructions are adhered to, we need not worry about the dilution of sound doctrine or divine order.

But as for you (Titus 2:1)

In the pastoral letters Paul has a habit of pointing out what is becoming the norm for many who profess to be preachers, teachers, and spiritual leaders. He compares the content of their teaching to the oracles of God, what God has actually said through divine inspiration. He also compares their behavior and way of life to the same. After he gives a description of their teaching, behavior, and lifestyle, he then charges Timothy and Titus concerning their doctrine and deportment. He uses phrases like "But as for you," "You then," "You however," and "As for you." These are all short phrases, but they speak volumes when it comes to knowing and doing the will of God. I believe that even now, God is looking at new church trends, fads, and passing ministry fancies, and saying to those who belong to Him, "But as for you, teach what accords with sound doctrine." I believe God is looking at the emphasis on material prosperity, worldliness, and the consumer mentality, and saying to those who are called and sent by Him, "But as for you, renounce ungodliness and worldly passions, live self-controlled, upright, and godly lives in this present age" (Titus 2:12). As a born-again believer, you are a chosen race, a royal priesthood, a holy nation, a people for His own possession. Let others do what they will. But as for you, know and do the will of God.

Show perfect courtesy toward all people
(Titus 3:2)

Every human being is created in the image and likeness of our Creator God. For this reason Christian believers should treat everyone with love, respect, and kindness. We often say that respect must be earned, but it is our responsibility to flesh out these Christian virtues toward all people. We treat people the way we want to be treated, even when they don't reciprocate.

Remember, Jesus interceded on behalf of His executioners. When He was reviled, He didn't revile in return. We should also guard our tongues when speaking of others. We will ruin our own reputations if we seek to ruin the reputation of others. I often say that attempted homicide will lead to suicide. Don't ever try to crush or destroy anyone for any reason because you end up doing it to yourself. We must show kindness to all people, not only to one another. We have to ask ourselves, "How do my actions affect those outside the household of faith?" Let your light shine before others, so that they may see your good works and give glory to your Father who is in heaven. (Matt. 5:16)

For I have derived much joy and comfort from your love, my brother, because the hearts of the saints have been refreshed through you. (Philem. 7)

Philemon was a beloved fellow worker of Paul, who opened his home to the saints as a place of worship. Paul was thankful to God for him and often prayed for him. The aged apostle had heard of the love he had for the saints, the faith he had toward Christ, and his willingness to share that faith. Paul had also received much joy and comfort from this spiritual brother because the hearts of the saints had been refreshed through him. The acts of kindness and encouragement we commit don't originate within us. God is always doing His work through us; we are simply instruments of His grace. It is not the will of God that we become reservoirs of His gracious blessings, but that we would be channels of blessings that flow to others as a source of refreshment. We all need times of refreshing. We are engaged in the daily affairs of life, along with the constant challenges brought on by spiritual warfare. And like David, we should be able to strengthen ourselves in the Lord during these trying and difficult times. But God will sometimes send a loving and compassionate brother or sister in Christ to refresh us. Like Philemon, which means "loving and affectionate," we should seek to bring joy, comfort, and refreshment to those who encounter us.

And He upholds the universe by the word of His power. (Heb. 1:3)

According to the apostle John, all things were made through Christ, and without Him was not any thing made that was made. (John 1:3) Jesus Christ, the Word, is the creator of all things. All things were created by the word of His power. He spoke and matter came into existence. But not only does He make, He also manages, maintains, and progressively moves forward what is made. The universe is totally sustained by the powerfully effective Word of our Lord and Savior Jesus Christ. Now that's power! But the same thing He does for His creation, He also does for His chosen. He said, "Follow Me and I will make you" (Matt. 4:19). Christians are new creatures in Christ Jesus. We have been made anew and are being made. He holds us up to keep us from falling down. He holds us together to keep us from falling apart. And He carries us along. This should give us the assurance of knowing that whatever we encounter or go through, God is there to see us through and to bring His plan for our lives to completion. Now let the church say *Amen.*

For because He Himself has suffered when tempted, He is able to help those who are being tempted. (Heb. 2:18)

Jesus was fully God and fully man. He was divine and human. When He became flesh and dwelt among us, He did not relinquish His divine attributes but simply lived under self-imposed restrictions. He felt physical and emotional pain just as we do. He experienced hunger, thirst, and physical exhaustion just as all mankind does. In His divinity, He always knows what we are going through, and in His humanity, He can always identify with what we are experiencing. Because He was a suffering Savior, He understands and identifies with our suffering. He even understands the suffering we feel in the midst of temptation. He Himself endured the suffering that accompanies temptation. He was tempted but never yielded, and because He never gave in to temptation, He felt its full force. Therefore, He is fully aware of the emotions involved. We sometimes yield to temptation, which alleviates some of the suffering that accompanies it. But we do suffer its consequences, sometimes during, and certainly afterward. Jesus can help us before, during, and after being tempted. Ask the Savior to help you. He has been there and done that.

Today, if you hear His voice, do not harden your
hearts as in the rebellion. (Heb. 3:15)

Hardening of the arteries occurs when fat, cholesterol, and other unhealthy substances build up in the walls of arteries. These deposits are called plagues. Over time, these plagues can narrow or completely block the arteries and cause problems throughout the body. Hardening of the arteries is progressive, happens over time, and does untold physical damage. Hardening of the heart is very similar. It occurs when one lives in constant rejection to the voice of God. God speaks in many ways, especially through His Word. When one is constantly exposed to the Word, workings, and wonders of God, and refuses to acknowledge Him as God, hardness sets in. The same sun that melts wax hardens clay. My pastor says, "The same sermon that causes Sister Smith to shout can cause Sister Jones to pout."

Hardening of the heart is progressive, occurs over time, and does eternal damage to one's soul. The hardhearted person is one who has constantly rejected all of God's advances over time. However God chooses to speak to you today, do not harden your heart in rebellion. Hear and heed His voice and live a life of spiritual health and wellness.

Let us then with confidence draw near to the
throne of grace, that we may receive mercy and
find grace to help in time of need. (Heb. 4:16)

God has enabled us to draw near to Him, receive mercy from Him, and find the seasonal grace needed to help us in our time of need. And we owe these awesome privileges to Jesus our great High Priest. It has always been the task of the priest to represent the people before God. When Christ ascended on high He sat down at the right hand of God the Father. There He ever lives to make intercession on our behalf.

Because of His position with the Father and His passion for His people, we can approach the throne of grace with all confidence in Him and His priestly ministry. Unlike earthly priests, He is able to sympathize and identify with our every weakness. He was tempted just as we are, yet without sin. We sometimes seek counsel, guidance, and other kinds of help from people who say that they understand. But do they really understand? When we go to our great High Priest, we are not concerned about being misunderstood. He completely understands and identifies with our every situation and circumstance.

When it comes to seeking the help we need, Christ should be our first choice, not our last resort. Let us humbly draw near to Him will all confidence. He is fully and perfectly aware of our needs.

He can deal gently with the ignorant and way-
ward, since he himself is beset with weakness.
(Heb. 5:2)

The priest was a spiritual leader among the children of Israel. As stated earlier, he represented the people before God. He had the responsibility of offering sacrifices on their behalf. Occupying the priestly office did not make him better than the people. He was made from the dust of the earth just as they were. He held the office because of divine appointment in spite of his own human imperfections. For this reason, he was obligated to offer sacrifices for his own sins just as he did for those of the people. When spiritual leaders constantly acknowledge, confess, and repent of their own sins, it enables them to deal gently with others concerning theirs. Spiritual leaders are experienced at hiding their own sin but are fully aware of its existence. Because of the consciousness of their own sin, they are compelled to be gentle with the ignorant and wayward church member. Possessing biblical knowledge is great, but knowledge can cause one to become proud, which leads to contempt for the biblically illiterate. It is possible for a spiritual leader to live in a backslidden condition, even while fulfilling his ministry responsibilities. Therefore, he should be gentle with the wayward as he deals with his own waywardness. The preacher's first woe should be "Woe is me!"

We have this as a sure and steadfast anchor of the soul, a hope that enters into the inner place behind the curtain. (Heb. 6:19)

We have this! What is this which we have as a sure and steadfast anchor of the soul? An anchor can be defined as a person or thing that can be relied on for support, stability, and security. The soul is the immortal, not material, part of man, the part of him that never dies. Also, in certain contexts, the soul is the person himself. Every soul is in need of a sure and steadfast anchor. What we have been given as an anchor of the soul is the blessed hope that is in us. Hope is one of the abiding sources of encouragement in the Christian life. This constant expectation of a favorable outcome serves as an anchor for the soul of every blood-bought believer. Without hope we die, but where there is life there is the possibility of hope, and where there is new life in Christ Jesus, there is an abiding hope of all that God has promised. When Jesus ascended to heaven, He entered into the presence of the Father in the Most Holy Place on our behalf. There He sits in the place of supreme privilege and authority. Because of who He is and what He's done, He is able to save completely and eternally. This gives us hope that serves as an anchor for the soul.

It is beyond dispute that the inferior is blessed by the superior. (Heb. 7:7)

Melchizedek is an Old Testament "type" of Christ. His priesthood is an illustration, a picture of the high priesthood of Christ. He is called priest of the Most High God. His kingship is also an example of the kingship of Christ. He is referred to as "king of righteousness" and "king of peace." When Melchizedek met the patriarch Abraham, he blessed him, and Abraham gave a tenth of everything to him.

Melchizedek, the superior, blessed Abraham, the inferior. Abraham, the inferior, gave a tenth to Melchizedek, the superior. We are familiar with the saying, "To the victor goes the spoils." This is often seen in the Old Testament after the Israelite army has defeated an enemy. Whenever God was with Israel, they were victorious in battle. God (the superior) blessed them (the inferior) in battle, and they (the inferior), according to the Mosaic Law, gave to God (the superior) what was rightfully His. As born-again believers, God has blessed us in Christ with every spiritual blessing in the heavenly places. And we would do well to remember that all blessings, temporal and spiritual, are bestowed on us by our gracious God.

All that we have and all that we are is because of Him. As He keeps on blessing us, we should keep on giving back to Him. This is beyond dispute.

For when Moses was about to erect the tent, he was instructed by God, saying, "See that you make everything according to the pattern that was shown you on the mountain" (Heb. 8:5).

God is the Creator of the entire universe. He spoke and the nonexistent began to exist. His creation is wonderfully, beautifully, and intelligently designed. Behind the intelligent design of the universe is the divine designer who possesses all intelligence. God designed every minute detail of His entire creation, insuring that it was indeed very good. When it comes to God, the details always matter. To Him, the small things always matter because the big picture is a combination of all the small things. When God commanded Moses to erect the tabernacle, He gave to him strict divine directions. No detail went unaddressed. In order for the tabernacle to be what God wanted, Moses had to give attention to detail as directed by God. Believe it or not, God is concerned about every aspect of our lives. The believer cannot live a compartmentalized Christian life. We cannot choose to obey God in the areas of our choosing and disobey Him in others. He has given to us precise biblical instruction for every aspect of our lives. When it comes to the way we live in His presence and in the presence of others, the details matter. Our attitudes, actions, and aims should be in accordance with what He has shown us in the biblical prescription.

So Christ, having been offered once to bear the sins of many, will appear a second time, not to deal with sin but to save those who are eagerly waiting for Him. (Heb. 9:28)

When Christ appeared the first time, His primary objective was to bear the sins of many. He fed the hungry, healed the sick, and raised the dead; but His main purpose was to offer Himself for the sins of the world. He spoke not as the scribes but as one having authority. When He spoke, the common people heard Him gladly, and never a man spoke like Him. But His main reason for coming was to give His life a ransom for many. He was the Lamb that was slain from the foundation of the world. No one took His life, but He gave it of His own accord. This is the work that God the Father assigned to Him so that we might have everlasting life. This was the purpose of His first coming. But when He returns the second time, it won't be for the purpose of offering Himself as our sin-bearer. At His second coming, believers will experience salvation in all its fullness. This is ultimate salvation: to be saved from the very presence of sin and to be totally conformed to the image of Christ. This is what we are eagerly awaiting. To see Him as He is and to be like Him is what we hope for with great anticipation.

*Waiting from that time until His enemies should
be made a footstool for His feet (Heb. 10:13)*

Even though the children of God don't always enjoy waiting for His plans to proceed, waiting is a part of the Christian life. We must remember that there is a time and a season for all things. Therefore we must wait for each season to come in its successive order. As we wait, our exalted Savior is also waiting. This present age in which we live is a waiting period, as Christ anticipates a final victory over His enemies.

When Christ had offered for all time a single sacrifice for sins, He sat down at the right hand of God. His sitting indicates a finished work, a one-time sacrifice, and the fact that He can now await the time when His enemies will be made His footstool. At that time, He will also establish His visible, righteous kingdom. At this present time, His throne is invisible, but at that time it will be visible for all to see. The enemies of Christ are presently under His sovereign rule but not in complete subjection to Him. But there is a day coming when every knee shall bow, in heaven and on earth, and under the earth, and every tongue confess that Jesus Christ is Lord, to the glory of God the Father. (Phil.2:10-11) In the end, there will come a universe in which Christ is visibly supreme with His enemies beneath His feet. But for now, He waits, and we wait. The good news is, as it is written it shall be done.

By faith (Heb. 11:1)

Biblical faith is believing that God is who He says He is, and that he will do what He says He will do. It is trusting and believing God. Biblical faith also involves attaching oneself to God. God is not one to be used during times of need and want by those who are not attached to Him through faith in the Lord Jesus Christ. When we exercise genuine saving faith, we attach ourselves to God, a relationship is established, and He becomes our Father and we become His children. From that point forward we begin to reverence, honor, and serve Him exclusively. As a result, He takes responsibility for our welfare. But one other thing needs to be emphasized. Genuine saving faith always leads to obedient actions. In the 11th chapter of Hebrews, the emphasis is on what the people of God did "by faith." It's about their trust and belief, their attachment to God, and their obedience to Him.

Eighteen times in this chapter we read "By faith." One time in this chapter we read "By it." Two times in this chapter we read "Through his faith." A person may say that they believe and trust God; that they are attached to Him. But the acid test of obedient action is what makes the difference. If your name was included in the faith hall of fame, what would follow the words "By faith?"

Consider Him who endured from sinners such hostility against Himself, so that you may not grow weary or fainthearted. (Heb. 12:3)

Believers are never without a well from which they can draw strength and encouragement. All of us experience times of difficulty, defeat, and discouragement. But God does not leave us to our own devices in times such as these. One of the wells from which we can draw is our own personal relationship with the Lord. On one occasion David's men spoke of stoning him, which caused him to become greatly distressed. But David strengthened himself in the Lord his God. (1 Sam. 30:6) He was able to press on through communion with God. Another well from which we can draw is the example of faith, obedience, and endurance seen in those who have gone on before us. The author of Hebrews reminds us of the "great cloud of witnesses" who are mentioned in the previous chapter. We can receive inspiration by considering the godly lives they lived. And of course, we can always draw strength and encouragement from the life of Christ. He is the prime example of endurance in the face of hostility, ridicule, blasphemy, and physical assault. He knew no sin but endured cruelty from sinners. He came to die for the very sinners who mistreated Him. When facing the cup of suffering and agony, He said, "Nevertheless, not My will, but Your will be done" (Luke 22:42). Consider Jesus and be strengthened and encouraged.

For He has said, "I will never leave you nor forsake you" (Heb. 13:5).

The children of God have no reason to worry. Our English word, *worry*, is equivalent to the combination of two Greek words, the first meaning "to divide" and the second meaning "mind." Worry really means "to divide the mind." A double-minded man is unstable in all his ways. (James 1:8)

When we are double-minded, we resemble a monster with two heads facing in opposite directions. We are also like a wave of the sea, driven and tossed by the wind. There are enough assurances in the Bible to remind us that we have no reason to worry, ever. God has promised, "I will never leave you nor forsake you" (Deut. 31:8). As we travel this road called life, He is our constant companion. I was always taught that a man's word was his bond. We have confidence in God because of what He has said. God will never withdraw His presence or His provision. And because of this promise, we can say with confidence, "The Lord is my helper; I will not fear. What can man do to me" (Heb. 13:6)? Because of our confidence in Him, we have no fears or phobias. We are not alarmed, frightened, or afraid. Where does our help come from? Our help comes from the Lord, who made heaven and earth. (Ps. 121:2) If God is for us, who can be against us? (Rom. 8:31)

Do not be deceived...deceiving yourselves...
deceives his heart (James 1:16, 22, 26)

It is obvious from the second half of chapter one that James, the half-brother of Jesus, is concerned about deception. He is concerned about the deception that often accompanies temptation. He makes it abundantly clear that God does not tempt us with evil, but we are lured and enticed by our own desires. Make no mistake about it, Satan is called a deceiver and is referred to as the tempter. For us to pursue what God has forbidden is sin and comes with grave consequences. Every good gift and every perfect gift is from above, coming down from the Father. (James 1:17) Do not be deceived! James is also concerned about the deception of false and incorrect reasoning on our part. We sometimes talk ourselves into sinning. For one to constantly hear the Word while failing to do the Word is self-deception. To look into a mirror and see ourselves as we really are without making the necessary changes is self-deception. Do not deceive yourself! Finally, James is concerned about the deception of outward ritual and ceremony devoid of internal godliness. When faith, belief, trust, and the worship of God is genuine, it will affect our speech. As we become the kind of worshipers that the Father is seeking, we begin to keep a tighter rein on our tongues. The condition of the inner man (heart) is often revealed by one's speech. Do not deceive your heart!

For judgment is without mercy to one who has shown no mercy. Mercy triumphs over judgment. (James 2:13)

We are often quick to judge the sins of others while overlooking our own. Even though all sin is not the same, all unrighteousness is still sin. James says, "For whoever keeps the whole law but fails in one point has become guilty of all of it" (James 2:10). This statement serves as an indictment against all of us. Since all of us are guilty of sin and in need of God's mercy, we should be merciful toward others. Loving your neighbor as yourself includes showing mercy. We often hear of someone's sinful behavior and respond by saying, "Lord have mercy!" But we are not asking for mercy. Instead, we are expressing our disgust with the sin and the sinner. The Lord has proven to be merciful, kind, and forgiving; we should follow His example. Jesus said, "Why do you see the speck that is in your brother's eye, but do not notice the log that is in your own eye? Or how can you say to your brother, 'Let me take the speck out of your eye,' when there is the log in your own eye? You hypocrite, first take the log out of your own eye, and then you will see clearly to take the speck out of your brother's eye" (Matt. 7:3-5). Blessed are the merciful, for they shall receive mercy. (Matt. 5:7)

But the wisdom from above is first pure, then peaceable, gentle, open to reason, full of mercy and good fruits, impartial and sincere. (James 3:17)

James describes the wisdom that does not come from above. This so-called wisdom produces bitter jealousy and selfish ambition in the heart. It is also the root of disorder and every vile practice. It is of the earth, unspiritual, and demonic. But there is a wisdom that's from above. Every good gift and every perfect gift is from above, and wisdom is one of these gifts. If any of us lacks wisdom, we should ask God, who gives generously to all without reproach. (James 1:5) The wisdom from above is spiritually genuine and morally sincere. It is motivated by what is true, right, and best. This wisdom is peace-loving rather than belligerent. The person who possesses this wisdom is reasonable, unselfish, easy to get along with, and of a humble spirit. It is merciful, forgiving, full of compassion, and spiritually fruitful. Finally, this wisdom is impartial and sincere. It describes a person who lives by the courage of his convictions, and exercises fairness with all people. Most of us consider ourselves wise; but do we really measure up?

You adulterous people! Do you not know that friendship with the world is enmity with God? Therefore, whoever wishes to be a friend of the world makes himself an enemy of God. (James 4:4)

With whom do you wish to be friends? Or maybe the question should be, "With what system do you wish to become friends?" We can't choose our relatives, but we can choose our friends. As a boy, my mother warned me about the dangers of running with the wrong crowd. Paul said, "Bad company ruins good morals" (1 Cor. 15:33). Every potential friend is connected to a system; either the evil world system, or what Elton Trueblood called "the company of the committed." Believers must beware of committing spiritual adultery. Adultery is always a dangerous endeavor, especially when it is of the spiritual kind. Many professing believers have a strong emotional attachment to the world and the things of the world. This is not good or spiritually profitable. Satan continues to convince weak, informed and uninformed believers that God does not mean what He says.

And to make matters worse, the average church is so concerned about popularity, likeability, and seeker-sensitivity, that it doesn't say much about sin, judgment, or hell. Many churches have become religious entertainment centers where everything goes, and no one is held accountable for anything. These things ought not to be so.

Behold, the wages of the laborers who mowed your fields, which you kept back by fraud, are crying out against you, and the cries of the harvesters have reached the ears of the Lord of hosts. (James 5:4)

Jesus said, "For you always have the poor with you" (Matt. 26:11). Many of the prosperity preachers teach that it is a sin for Christians to be poor. But being poor is a sin only if laziness is the cause of your poverty. People live in poverty for many different and complex reasons. Some people live in poverty because of economic injustice in the workplace. I recall as a boy, hearing people say, "An honest day's work for an honest day's pay." This sounds good and even makes good sense. But the problem is that so many poor people are among the working poor. They are slaving for scraps and unable to make ends meet, while the rich continue to get richer. In many instances, they are unappreciated, undervalued, and underpaid in order that their oppressive employers might live in the lap of luxury. This type of oppression and fraud is condemned by God. Imagine having money in your possession that cries out against you because it rightfully belongs to the employees you have defrauded. All money is not good money. The cries of oppressed laborers ultimately reach the ears of the Lord of hosts. The Lord of hosts is the name for God in His role as commander of the armies of heaven. The Lord hears their cries and will do what He wills.

He has caused us to be born again to a living hope through the resurrection of Jesus Christ from the dead. (1 Pet. 1:3)

There are theologians who refer to God as the "Uncaused Cause." This is based on the fact that God is the cause of creation, yet He Himself has always existed, therefore uncaused. From everlasting to everlasting, He is God; the Alpha and the Omega, the beginning and the ending. When we consider regeneration, being born from above, God is the cause of our new birth in Christ Jesus. Prior to His causing us to be born again, we were dead in trespasses and sins. We were following Satan, the god of this world, the prince of the power of the air, and were by nature the children of wrath. But God being rich in mercy because of the great love with which He loved us, made us alive together with Christ. By grace He has saved us through faith. This is not our own doing; it is the gift of God. (Eph. (2:1-5) He is the cause of our redemption. We have nothing to boast about. He is the cause of the living hope that is within us. He is the cause of Christ being raised from the dead. He will also cause our mortal bodies to put on immortality.

Therefore, we wait expectantly for Him because He is the Uncaused Cause.

> *By His wounds you have been healed. For you*
> *were straying like sheep but have now returned*
> *to the Shepherd and Overseer of your souls. (1*
> *Pet. 2:24–25)*

The prophet Isaiah predicted that the Messiah would heal people of their physical ailments. Isaiah 53:4 says, "He took our illnesses and bore our diseases." This prophecy was fulfilled during the Lord's earthly ministry as He went about performing miracles of mercy (Matt. 8:17). This He did as signs that pointed to something more significant than the miracles themselves. What was more significant than the healing of our physical ailments was the healing our sin-sickness. Isaiah prophesied about this as well; for he says in 53:5, "But He was wounded for our transgressions; He was crushed for our iniquities; upon Him was the chastisement that brought us peace, and with His stripes we are healed." This prophecy was not fulfilled during the Lord's ministry of healing physical sickness; it was fulfilled as He was tortured on the cross. He was wounded for our transgressions on the cross. He was bruised for our iniquities on the cross.

Upon Him was the chastisement that brought us peace. We have peace with God and peace within because of His suffering on the cross. Our spiritual healing was secured by His suffering on the cross. We were straying like sheep but have now returned to the Shepherd and Overseer of our souls.

But even if you should suffer for righteousness'
sake, you will be blessed. Have no fear of them,
nor be troubled. (1 Pet. 3:14)

To be blessed, in one sense, means to be "approved of"
or "spoken well of." This is not the prominent idea of being
blessed in this day and time. Most people think only in terms
of material possessions, financial prosperity, and physical and
mental health. These things are also associated with the world's
idea of what it means to be successful. To be clear, God can and
does bless His children with the material, financial, and physical. But there is so much more to the Christian life. Peter tells
us that there is a kind of blessing that comes from suffering
for righteousness' sake. This kind of blessing cannot be measured by cars, cash, and cabins in the country. When believers
are faithful to the Word and will of God at all costs, it often
involves suffering. When believers stand with and for Christ
in the face of opposition and ostracism, suffering is par for
the course. If we are committed to doing the Lord's will we
shouldn't be surprised by the suffering that follows. But the
good news is "you will be blessed." The apostle Peter is simply
saying to us that when we suffer for righteousness' sake, we
are "privileged" and "honored." Jesus said, "Rejoice and be glad,
for great is your reward in heaven, for so they persecuted the
prophets who were before you" (Matt. 5:12). That puts us in
pretty good company.

Therefore, be self-controlled and sober-minded
for the sake of your prayers. (1 Pet. 4:7)

The Bible often shares with us the great feats of faith and the victories won by God's servants. But the Bible doesn't stop there; it sometimes shares with us their failures as well. And many times they failed in the area in which they were known for their strength. All of God's children experience failure from time to time, and the apostle Peter was no different. Concerning Peter, he denied the Lord three times, and was restored by the Lord three times. I believe Peter's failure was connected to his prayerlessness, and so is ours. Jesus said to Peter, "So could you not watch (keep awake) with me one hour? Watch and pray that you may not enter into temptation" (Matt. 26:40). Jesus said on another occasion, "But stay awake (be spiritually alert) at all times, praying that you may have strength" (Luke 21:36). If Peter had been watching and praying at the appointed time, he wouldn't have done the wrong thing at the wrong time. Of course Jesus's prophecy had to be fulfilled, but Peter was still responsible. This applies to us as well. As believers, we must be spiritually alert and sober-minded that we might keep our appointments with God for communion through prayer.

A witness of the sufferings of Christ, as well as a
partaker in the glory that is going to be revealed
(1 Pet. 5:1)

Simon Peter was a simple fisherman who was called by Christ to become a fisher of men. He was one of the twelve disciples who were chosen to be with Christ. He was a member of the Lord's inner circle along with James and John, and was the leader of the twelve. Peter as well as the others would receive power on the Day of Pentecost and become the Lord's witnesses in Jerusalem, Judea, Samaria, and to the ends of the earth. A witness is one who has seen, heard, and experienced something. A witness is also one who tells what was seen, heard, and experienced. Jesus said to the disciples after His resurrection, "Everything written about Me in the Law of Moses and the Prophets, and the Psalms must be fulfilled." Then He opened their minds to understand the Scriptures, and said to them, "Thus it is written, that the Christ should suffer and on the third day rise from the dead...You are witnesses of these things" (Luke 24:44-48). Simon Peter was an eyewitness of the Lord's life and ministry. He witnessed the good, the bad, and the ugly. But he also got a glimpse of the Lord's glory on the mountain of transfiguration. Christ suffered, bled, and died; then came the exaltation and the glory. We must also suffer, but then comes the glory that shall be revealed in and to us. First, we suffer with Him; then we reign with Him. It really is worth it all.

I think it right, as long as I am in this body, to
stir you up by way of reminder. (2 Pet. 1:13)

Constant review is the teacher's glue, and repetition leads to retention. I learned these maxims in middle school. As pastors, we learn and teach; we teach and learn. In the teaching ministry, there are times of new discovery, but we are mostly reminding people of what has already been taught. Many times, what has been taught is not learned until it has been reviewed and repeated.

Sometimes the light is on, but nobody's home. After Peter's denial and restoration, He was commanded by the Lord, "When you have turned again, strengthen your brothers" (Luke 22:32). He was also commanded to feed the Lord's sheep and lambs. Afterward, the Lord prophesied concerning the death that Peter would die. As Peter writes this second epistle, he knows that the putting off of his body will be soon, as the Lord made clear to him. Now he is determined to make every effort so that after his departure, his readers may be able at any time to recall his teachings. Any sermon worth preaching is worth preaching again. Any lesson worth teaching is worth teaching again. We are often astonished when we discover that the people who sit under our teaching don't know what we thought they knew. Let's continue to stir them up by way of reminder.

There will be false teachers among you, who will
secretly bring in destructive heresies. (2 Pet. 2:1)

For everything that God has, Satan has a counterfeit. In days of old, there were prophets who were sent by God to deliver His message. But there were also false prophets who were sent by Satan to deliver a message that was different from that of the true prophets. The prophecies of God's prophets always came to pass, while those of the false prophets never did. Today there are pastor-teachers sent by God, and there are pastor-teachers sent by Satan. My childhood pastor would say that Satan doesn't wear red leotards with a pitchfork. And he would describe Satan as a nice-looking, well-dressed, polite, smooth-talking individual. Because of these outward attractions, false teachers are able to secretly bring in destructive heresies and lead people astray. Remember, the serpent was more crafty than any other beast of the field, and he deceived Eve. Heresy is a position or doctrine at variance with established, orthodox church doctrine. Peter refers to the doctrine of the false teachers as "destructive heresies." This language implies a willful departure from accepted teaching and the spiritual damage it does to the unsuspecting.

My brothers and sisters, there is an abundance of heretical teaching in the church today. However, it is so subtle that it goes unnoticed by the uninformed. Test and prove everything by the Word of God.

I am stirring up your sincere mind by way of reminder, that you should remember the predictions of the holy prophets and the commandments of the Lord and Savior through your apostles. (2 Pet. 3:1–2)

As previously stated, Peter was commanded by the Lord to strengthen the brothers and sisters, and to feed the Lord's sheep and lambs. As an apostle and author of two New Testament epistles, he received new revelation from God, but here he is moved to simply remind them of what they already knew. Peter was aware of the existence and influence of false prophets and false teachers, as well as scoffers who made light of the return of Christ and eternal judgment. These unbelievers lived as though there was no judgment, and as though Christ was still dead, never to be seen again. They even mocked believers for their anticipation of these future events. But Peter encouraged them to remember. The Old Testament prophets predicted the coming of our Lord and Savior Jesus Christ: His birth, death, and resurrection. They also had much to say about judgment and the second coming of the Lord. In the pages of the New Testament, the Lord's apostles often refer to His return, the gathering of the church, and the judgment of all mankind.

Let the heathen say what they will. But we must remember the Word of the Lord. Our God is in heaven; He does all that He pleases; when and where and with whom He pleases.

Concerning the Word of life...the eternal life,
which was with the Father and was made man-
ifest to us (1 John 1:1–2)

In the Gospel according to John, the apostle declares that Jesus is the eternal Word. He was in the beginning, He was with God, and He was God. (John 1:1-2) Now in the apostle John's first epistle, he refers to Jesus as the "Word of life." Jesus Christ is the life-giving Word.

The words that proceed from the mouth of the Word are spirit, and they are life. The Word of life came that we might have life and have it abundantly. John also refers to Jesus as "the eternal life," who was with the Father. Here John is placing emphasis on the eternality of Christ who dwelt in the bosom of the Father in eternity past until He was made manifest in the flesh. John assures us that he and the other apostles saw Him with their own eyes, heard Him with their own ears, and touched Him with their own hands before and after His death, burial, and resurrection. Now the Word of life is proclaimed to all people everywhere so that they may have fellowship with the Father and with His Son Jesus Christ.

What a fellowship!

Many antichrists have come. They went out from us, but they were not of us; for if they had been of us, they would have continued with us. But they went out, that it might become plain that they all are not of us. (1 John 2:18–19)

Apostasy is defined as "a falling away." Apostates are people who were affiliated with the church but were never saved, and eventually separated themselves from it. John shares with his readers the truth that many antichrists are in this world. Anti is a prefix which means "against" or "opposite of." Antichrists are against and opposed to Christ, His Word, and His church. John says, "Many antichrists have come." But what is interesting and alarming is the truth that they went out from us (the church). These apostates who are antichrist, anti-Bible, and anti-church, were at one time a part of a local congregation. And you can be sure that their antichristian attitudes and actions showed up from time to time while they were members of some church. But John says, "but they were not of us." In other words, they were never saved. Had they been saved, they would have continued with the church. Their leaving the church and being antichrist and opposed to everything that He represents made it obvious that they were never saved. A born-again believer can never become unborn again. Genuine believers worship with other believers, and they endure to the very end. Jesus saves completely and eternally.

We should not be like Cain, who was of the evil one and murdered his brother. And why did he murder him? Because his own deeds were evil and his brother's righteous. (1 John 3:12)

Cain and Abel came from the same womb. They had the same parents and the same upbringing. But they did not have the same spiritual father. Abel was righteous and had God as his heavenly Father. Cain was evil and had the devil as his hellish father. We should not be like Cain. Cain was a hypocrite; He pretended to be something that he was not. He even offered a sacrifice to God. But he did not offer what was required, and his heart wasn't right before God. Therefore, God rejected Cain and his sacrifice. Abel also offered a sacrifice to God, and God accepted him and his sacrifice. As a result of God's acceptance of Abel and his sacrifice, Cain was overcome with anger and murdered him. I believe Cain was angry with God and his brother. But he couldn't kill God. Cain was also jealous of Abel. Abel's righteous life was an open rebuke to Cain's evil way of life. Cain hated Abel, and everyone who hates his brother is a murderer, and you know that no murderer has eternal life abiding in him. (1 John 3:15) This is the message that you have heard from the beginning, that we should love one another. (1 John 3:11) We know that we have passed out of death into life because we love the brothers. (1 John 3:14)

For He who is in you is greater than he who is in the world. (1 John 4:4)

Once again, the apostle John warns believers about false prophets and false teachers. He says, "Beloved, do not believe every spirit, but test the spirits to see whether they are from God" (1 John 4:1). During His last days with the apostles, Jesus promised to send the Holy Spirit, who is the Spirit of truth. The Holy Spirit would teach them all things, and bring to their remembrance all that Jesus had spoken to them. He would take what was Christ's and declare it to them. The Holy Spirit would indeed be their Helper, Teacher, and Comforter. This is the same Holy Spirit who indwells (lives inside of) every born-again believer. God the Son is in us; God the Holy Spirit is in us. The divine Person who indwells us is greater than he who is in the world. There are many antichrists in the world; but He is greater. False prophets and false teachers who operate under the influence of demonic spirits are in the world; but He is greater.

Satan himself is in the world; but God is greater. The indwelling Holy Spirit enables us to wise up to the Word of God, which equips us to overcome the destructive heresies and doctrines of demons propagated by the false prophets and teachers. God the Son gave His Word to the apostles in the days of His flesh. After His ascension, He gave to them His Word through the ministry of the Holy Spirit. This is the Word they were commissioned to give to the church. This is the authoritative Word that God's people are called to believe and live by. If it's new, it ain't true; if it's true, it ain't new.

For everyone who has been born of God over-
comes the world. And this is the victory that has
overcome the world, our faith. Who is it that
overcomes the world except the one who believes
that Jesus is the Son of God? (1 John 5:4–5)

Every born-again child of God overcomes the world. The world, in this context, has been defined as a system of deception and wickedness, led by Satan, that opposes everything that Christ represents. To have new life in Christ Jesus is to be in the world but not of it. This is what it means to be an overcomer. Overcomers don't allow the world to squeeze them into its mold. Overcomers are not conformists; allowing the spirit of the age to dictate to them their beliefs and practices. The apostle Paul said, "Do not be conformed to this world, but be transformed by the renewing of your mind, that by testing you may discern what is the will of God, what is good and acceptable and perfect" (Rom. 12:2). Genuine saving faith and a life of persevering through faith is what enables believers to live the victorious Christian life. The apostle Paul also said, "From faith to faith; the just shall live by his faith" (Rom. 1:17). This is faith and faith alone, faith from beginning to end. We believe by faith that Jesus is who the Bible says He is. By this, we overcome the world.

Whoever abides in the teaching has both the
Father and the Son. (2 John 9)

Jesus said, "If you abide in My word, you are truly My disciples, and you will know the truth, and the truth will set you free" (John 8:31). He also said, "I am the vine; you are the branches. Whoever abides in Me and I in him, he it is that bears much fruit, for apart from Me you can do nothing" (John 15:5). Jesus is the truth; His word is truth. Abiding in His Word leads to the knowledge of the truth, and the knowledge of the truth leads to true freedom and fruit-bearing. And apart from Him we can do nothing. The evidence of having the Father and the Son is abiding in the teaching, which is the truth we have been given in the pages of the Holy Bible. Everyone who goes on ahead and does not abide in the teaching of Christ does not have God. Whoever abides in the teaching has both the Father and the Son. The most important teaching is the teaching about Christ. He is the Son of God who came in the flesh. He did die for the sins of the world. He was raised from the grave early on the third day's morning. He ascended back to heaven and is seated at the right hand of the Father in glory. He ever lives to make intercession for the saints, and one day He will return. Do not be deceived, but abide in His teaching.

Beloved, do not imitate evil but imitate good.
Whoever does good is from God; whoever does
evil has not seen God. (3 John 11)

There are three noted personalities in John's third epistle. Two of these personalities are worthy of imitation, and one is not. In his fatherly tone, the aged apostle reminds his beloved children to imitate good and not evil. Based on the record of their attitudes and activities, it is easy to discern which is worthy of imitation. Gaius, which means, "rejoice," is the addressee of this epistle. He was commended by the apostle for his generosity and faithfulness in serving God and the church. He was loved by John, and the apostle desired his continued support for missionaries.

Diotrephes, which means, "nourished by Jupiter/Zeus," was an unruly church member who had to be reprimanded by John. In Scripture, names have significance, and the meaning of his name explains a lot. He loved to have the preeminence, making everything about him. His was a strong and domineering personality that rejected the authority of divinely-appointed church leadership. His desire was for power and dominance over the congregation. But then there is Demetrius. He was commended by everyone in the local congregation, and the apostle commended him as well. Which of these is worthy of imitation?

I found it necessary to write appealing to you to contend for the faith that was once for all delivered to the saints. (Jude 3)

Sometimes our desires and God's directions are totally different. This is where we say, "Not my will but Your will be done." Jude had an eager desire to write to the recipients of this letter about their common salvation. Had his desire been fulfilled, he would have talked about the joy of being loved and saved by the grace of God. He would have spoken of being redeemed and bought with a price. Perhaps he would have written about the Lord's power to deliver from sin and the penalty of sin. All of this would have been good, but this is not what God directed him to pen. As a result of being moved and directed by the Holy Spirit, he found it necessary to write appealing to them to contend for the faith that was once for all delivered to the saints. Jude's eagerness was good, but the Holy Spirit's urging was the will of God. The faith that Jude speaks of is the Christian faith and all that it embodies in the teachings of the Holy Bible. Satan's attacks take place on the battlefield of the mind. Therefore, it is God's will that our minds be always prepared for action in accordance with the teachings of Scripture. The experts in the area of apologetics will contend by fulfilling their ministries. The rest of us should always be prepared to make a defense to anyone who asks us for a reason for the hope that is in us. (1 Pet. 3:15) Know what you believe and why you believe it, and be able to defend and contend.

And from Jesus Christ the faithful witness, the firstborn of the dead, and the ruler of kings on the earth (Rev. 1:5)

The one in whom we have placed our trust is none other than Jesus who is the Christ. Prior to the birth of Jesus, the angel said to Joseph, "And you shall call His name Jesus, for He will save His people from their sins" (Matt. 1:21). Jesus means "Savior," and He is the Savior of all who believe. Jesus is the Christ (Messiah, Anointed One). He is the one spoken of in the Old Testament who will destroy the rulers of this world, deliver Israel from her enemies, and restore her as a nation. The Messiah will put an end to war, for He is the Prince of Peace and will rule in righteousness over His people. He is also the "faithful witness," the one who is the truth, and always speaks and represents the truth. Of all who have ever been or ever will be resurrected, He is the preeminent one. Others were raised from the dead, but eventually died again. He is the first to be resurrected from the dead never to die again. He is also Lord; ruler of the kings on the earth. It may not appear as though this is true at this time, but God is on the throne, and Jesus Christ is seated at His right hand. There is a day coming when His glory and dominion will be seen and experienced by all, whether in heaven, on the earth, or under the earth. We are grateful that He loves us and has freed us from our sins by His blood.

To the angel of the church...He who has an ear,
let him hear what the Spirit says to the churches
(Rev. 2:1, 7)

What Christ thinks of His church and what He says to it is of the utmost importance. He has a right to think and say what He does. In the first place, it is His church. He is its founder and builder, and promises that the gates of hell would not prevail against it. He is its head and the source of its life. In the second place, He knows His church intimately. In each of the seven letters He begins "I know." "I know your deeds, your hard work and your perseverance." He says, "I know your affliction and your poverty." "I know where you live." "I know your love and faith, your service and perseverance." He walks among the lampstands (churches), patrolling and supervising. He is the Chief Shepherd of His people. He addresses each letter to the "angel" of the church, who is the pastor. When citizens band (CB) radios were really popular, each user had a handle, which was a name that was used while communicating with other users. To see if a user's radio was on, the question was always asked, "You got your ears on?" If your ears were on, you could communicate with other users who were on the same channel and a short distance away. For us to hear what the Spirit is saying, we must have our spiritual ears on, stay close, and operate on the same channel. Pastors and people need to hear what the Spirit is saying to the churches. Are your ears on?

Behold, I stand at the door and knock. If anyone
hears My voice and opens the door, I will come
in to him and eat with him, and he with Me.
(Rev. 3:20)

The New Testament call to salvation is always a call to repentance. And since it is time for judgment to begin at the household of God, those whose names are recorded on the church roll should be the first to repent. It is a sad sight to see Jesus standing at the door of the church, knocking and offering intimate fellowship to those on the inside. Jesus offers Himself to all but will force Himself on no one. This scene causes one to wonder if the church at Laodicea consisted of few believers or any at all. They considered themselves rich and prosperous, but were spiritually bankrupt. They were void of the true riches of salvation. They were known for their famed black wool, which represented their spiritual filthiness and nakedness. But Christ offers to clothe them in white garments that symbolized purity. Laodicea was known for its eye salve that was developed at its medical school, but spiritual sight and insight was what they really needed. Some people love their own idea or concept of the church, but not the church that Christ said He would build. Any house of worship where Christ is not welcome is not a church. But if we listen to Him and are open to Him, He will come in and fellowship with us.

Worthy are You, our Lord and God, to receive glory and honor and power, for You created all things, and by Your will they existed and were created. (Rev. 4:11)

The apostle Paul was caught up to the third heaven, which is the abode of God. There he was given a glimpse of glory but was not permitted to speak concerning what he witnessed. On the other hand, while exiled on the island of Patmos, the apostle John was empowered by the Holy Spirit to witness heavenly activities and write about them. As his Spirit-enhanced senses allowed him to see, hear, and experience the glories of heaven, he heard the voice of Jesus telling him to write what he saw in a book. As he looked and listened, he observed worship unlike anything he had ever seen. There he saw a throne with one who sat on it. Around the throne were twenty-four thrones, and twenty-four elders seated on them, clothed in white garments, with golden crowns on their heads. Around the throne, there were four living creatures who day and night never cease to say, "Holy, holy, holy, is the Lord God Almighty, who was and is and is to come" (Rev. 4:8)! As a response to the praise and worship of the four living creatures, the twenty-four elders would fall down and worship Him who was on the throne, casting their crowns before the throne, speaking of His worthiness to be worshiped. In heaven, elders rise from their seats, fall on their faces, and cast their crowns before Him. In heaven, living creatures never cease to praise Him day and night. The lessor gives praise to the greater, in heaven and on earth. Let everything that has breath praise the Lord! Praise the Lord! (Ps. 150:6)

*And I heard every creature in heaven and on
earth and under the earth and in the sea, and
all that is in them, saying, "To Him who sits
on the throne and to the Lamb be blessing and
honor and glory and might forever and ever"
(Rev. 5:13)!*

Philippians 2:9–11 says, "Therefore God has highly
exalted Him and bestowed on Him the name that is above
every name, so that at the name of Jesus every knee should
bow, in heaven and on earth and under the earth, and every
tongue confess that Jesus Christ is Lord, to the glory of God
the Father." As the apostle John continued to observe worship
in heaven, he noticed that other beings were now taking part
in the worship experience. Those who had joined in worship
had done so after the Lamb had taken the scroll from Him
who was seated on the throne. The Lamb was worthy to take
the scroll because He is "the Lamb of God who takes away the
sin of the world." The Lamb had taken the sin and was, therefore, qualified and worthy to take the scroll. He was standing
as though He has been slain. The twenty-four elders and the
four living creatures fell down before Him and worshipped.
The voice of many thousands of angels began to extol His worthiness. Finally, John began to observe worship, not only in
heaven, but on the earth and under the earth and in the sea,
and all of its inhabitants magnified the name of the Father and
Son. When God brings His eternal plan to fruition, every creature everywhere, including those who are under the earth experiencing eternal torment, will bend the knee and confess that
Jesus is Lord.

Open our eyes, now, Lord, that we might see Jesus.

*Calling to the mountains and rocks, "Fall on us
and hide us from the face of Him who is seated
on the throne, and from the wrath of the Lamb,
for the great day of their wrath has come, and
who can stand? (Rev. 6:16–17)*

The wrath of God is His necessary, just, and righteous retribution against sin. God does not take pleasure in punishing the unrighteous, but He will, because he is a God of wrath. We must remember that God is a God of love and a God of wrath. We must view both sides of His character. The apostle John observes that with the breaking of the sixth seal by the Lamb, God will send an earthquake more powerful and devastating than any in the history of the world. The sun will become as black as sackcloth, and the full moon will become like blood. There will also be asteroids or meteor showers bombarding the earth. The sky will be rolled up like a scroll, and the mountains and islands will be moved out of their places. John then describes the terror of an impenitent world. All classes of society make a futile attempt to escape God's punishment for their oppression and persecution of Christians, and rejection of Jesus Christ. They are not so much afraid of death as of the revealed presence of God and of the righteous anger of Christ. The scene closes with the asking of the rhetorical question, "Who is able to stand?" The answer is "No one." Let us thank and praise God for deliverance from the wrath to come.

Salvation belongs to our God who sits on the throne, and to the Lamb! (Rev. 7:10)

Salvation is deliverance from sin and the penalty of sin. The ultimate penalty of sin is eternal separation from God while experiencing the excruciating pain of hell. Those who have received God's free gift of salvation have been delivered from hell and all of its torment. Salvation was God's idea; it was birthed out of the love that He has for mankind. Therefore salvation belongs to God the Father and God the Son.

Revelation 7:9–17 describes the vast multitude of people from all the nations of the world who will be saved during the coming tribulation. This group is described as a great multitude which no one could number, from every nation, from all tribes and peoples and languages, standing before the throne and before the Lamb. They are crying out with a loud voice, "Salvation belongs to our God who sits on the throne, and to the Lamb!" These tribulation saints are in heaven, standing before the throne of God. They have washed their robes and made them white in the blood of the Lamb. The apostle Peter said, "And there is salvation in no one else, for there is no other name under heaven given among men by which we must be saved" (Acts 4:12). Jesus said, "I am the way, and the truth, and the life. No one comes to the Father except through Me" (John 14:6). Enough said.

Then I looked, and I heard an eagle crying with a loud voice as it flew directly overhead, "Woe, woe, woe to those who dwell on the earth, at the blasts of the other trumpets that the three angels are about to blow" (Rev. 8:13)!

The book of Revelation has always been a frightening book for many people. But it need not be a frightening read for the redeemed. In the very first chapter, the apostle John says, "Blessed is the one who reads aloud the words of this prophecy, and blessed are those who hear, and who keep what is written in it, for the time is near" (Rev. 1:3). The revealing of the consequences of certain actions and inactions can often serve as a deterrent to sins of commission and omission. The apostle John is given a first-hand look at the judgments that will precede the day of the Lord. At the blowing of the first four of the seven trumpets by the seven angels, cataclysmic destruction occurs in the heavens and on the earth. The word *woe* is used throughout Scripture as an expression of judgment, destruction, and condemnation. "Those who dwell on the earth" is an identifying phrase for those who reject Christ and the gospel message. There are three "woes" for the remaining three trumpet blasts. For the unbelievers, things will continue to get worse. Therefore, as the Holy Spirit says, "Today, if you hear His voice, do not harden your hearts as in the rebellion, on the day of testing in the wilderness" (Heb. 3:15). The saints are safe and secure, and need not worry or be afraid.

The rest of mankind, who were not killed by these plagues, did not repent of the works of their hands nor give up worshiping demons and idols of gold and silver and bronze and stone and wood, which cannot see or hear or walk, nor did they repent of their murders or their sorceries or their sexual immorality or their thefts. (Rev. 9:20–21)

John the Baptist, who was the forerunner of Jesus, came onto the scene preaching, "Repent, for the kingdom of heaven is at hand" (Matt. 3:2). Jesus also began to preach, saying, "Repent, for the kingdom of heaven is at hand" (Matt. 4:17). On the day of Pentecost, the apostles were asked, "Brothers, what shall we do?" Peter said to them, "Repent and be baptized every one of you in the name of Jesus Christ for the forgiveness of your sins, and you will receive the gift of the Holy Spirit" (Acts 2:38) Repentance is a voluntary and sincere change in the mind of the sinner, causing him to turn from his sin. Repentance (turning from sin) and faith (turning to God) results in conversion. But there are some who will never repent. When people have been given over to a reprobate mind, there is no turning back. But the Lord is patient, not wishing that any should perish, but that all should reach repentance. (2 Pet. 3:9) He knows that the hard-hearted will continue in their defiance of Him.

Yet He is longsuffering.

> *And I took the little scroll from the hand of the angel and ate it. It was sweet as honey in my mouth, but when I had eaten it my stomach was made bitter. (Rev.10:10)*

God's Word is sometimes compared to food. Jesus called it "bread." Peter refers to it as "milk." Paul calls it "meat." Like physical food, the Word of God must be eaten and internalized so it can produce spiritual life, health, and growth. Just as God stands at the door and knocks instead of forcing Himself into our lives and local churches, He doesn't force-feed His Word into us. But He makes it available to us, and we must choose to partake. When Ezekiel was called to the prophetic ministry, he was given a scroll and told to eat it. He did not literally eat the scroll, but in a spiritual sense he received the prophetic pronouncements that he would later deliver. God's message was in his mouth as sweet as honey, but he went in bitterness to deliver it to the Lord's people. (Ezek. 3:1-3) The apostle John had a similar experience. God's message to him was sweet as honey in his mouth, but his stomach was made bitter. In receiving and delivering God's messages, His messengers will experience both joy and sorrow, sweetness and bitterness. We are joyful and glad about what God has in store for His children, even as we are sorrowful about the future judgment of lost sinners.

> *And those who dwell on the earth will rejoice over them and make merry and exchange presents, because these two prophets had been a torment to those who dwell on the earth. (Rev. 11:10)*

God's preachers/prophets are not friends of the evil world system. Because of their divine calling and appointment, they are indeed enemies of the world. Jesus said, "If the world hates you, know that it has hated Me before it hated you" (John 15:18). Throughout history God has faithfully dispatched His preacher/prophets to call sinners to repentance. God sent the Old Testament prophets to confront wayward Israel and sinful Gentile nations. In the future, God will raise up two powerful and fearless preachers who will faithfully proclaim His message during the last half of the seven-year tribulation. The death of these faithful witnesses will occur after they have completed their assignment. While I am certain there will be mourning among the saints, this won't be the mood of "those who dwell on the earth," a phrase used to speak of unbelievers. Instead, they will rejoice, celebrate, and exchange presents with one another as if it were a holiday. Their bodies will be left to rot in the street for all the world to see. But after three and one-half days, God will raise them up and call them up to heaven in a cloud, with their enemies watching. On earth, He prepares a table for us in the presence of our enemies. In heaven, our enemies won't be a concern of ours. They will spend eternity in the place prepared for them, and we will spend eternity in the place prepared for us. God has the first and the last word. Praise His holy name!

But he was defeated...The great dragon was
thrown down...And they have conquered him
(Rev. 12:8, 9, 11)

Satan has a perfect losing record in all of his skirmishes with God's kingdom in heaven and on earth. He is the biggest loser of all time and throughout eternity. He lost the war in heaven after attempting to usurp God's position and power. He, along with his horde of angelic followers, were defeated and thrown down to earth. There was no longer any place for them in heaven.

Heaven doesn't permit beings of dragon-like character to dwell there. This is the serpent who deceived Eve, who is called the devil and Satan. He is the deceiver of the whole world. He is also the accuser of the brothers and sisters; he accuses them day and night before God. He is not omniscient, but he does possess knowledge of some things. One thing he knows is that his time is short; it is running out. Therefore, with his remaining time he seeks to steal, kill, and destroy as much as the Lord will allow. But the saints are on the winning side, the side that has a perfect winning record in all of its battles with Satan. The saints are victorious over him by the blood of the Lamb and by the word of their testimony. Satan is a fallen angel who became the devil. He is a defeated foe who knows that his days are numbered. Put on the whole armor of God and resist him, steadfast in the faith. (Eph. 6:11; 1 Pet. 5:9) Be faithful unto death, and Christ will give you the crown of life. (Rev. 2:10)

And all who dwell on the earth will worship
it, everyone whose name has not been written
before the foundation of the world in the book
of life of the Lamb that was slain. (Rev. 13:8)

Every human being is created to worship, and every human being is a worshiper. Remember, in the book of Revelation, "those who dwell on the earth" is a phrase that refers to unbelievers.

Unbelievers do not worship God, and if a person doesn't worship God he is capable of worshiping anything and anybody. This is plainly seen in the second half of the tribulation. At that time, unbelievers will worship the dragon who is Satan. Not only will they worship the dragon, they will also worship the beast who is the Antichrist. The Antichrist will utter blasphemies against God, blaspheming His name and those who dwell in heaven. Yet the unbelievers of the world will worship him. The unbelievers of the world will marvel at and follow the beast, saying, "Who is like the beast, and who can fight against it" (Rev. 13:4)? The beast will be allowed to make war on the saints and to conquer them. And the unbelievers of the world will continue to worship him. The only inhabitants of the earth who won't worship the dragon and the beast will be those whose names are written in the Lamb's book of life. The Lamb was slain and raised from the dead. Many of those who worship Him at this time will be slain and eventually raised from the dead. Worshiping God has always been costly for true worshipers. But we've read the rest of the story, and it is worth the cost. Here is a call for the endurance and faith of the saints. (Rev. 13:10)

> *Then I saw another angel flying directly over-*
> *head, with an eternal gospel to proclaim to*
> *those who dwell on earth, to every nation and*
> *tribe and language and people. (Rev. 14:6)*

The gospel is the good news about the death, burial, and resurrection of Jesus Christ. It is the only message that can draw one to eternal life in Christ Jesus. Therefore, it is an eternal gospel. Even during the tribulation period and world-wide reign of the Antichrist, the gospel will be preached and people will be saved. Again, in the book of Revelation, "those who dwell on earth" is a reference to unbelievers. God cannot and will not change; therefore, He is not wishing that any should perish, but that all should reach repentance. (2 Pet. 3:9) Time will eventually run out for everyone, but at this point in redemptive history, the door to salvation is beginning to close for all eternity. The angel exhorts "those who dwell on earth" to reverence and respect God, to give Him glory, and to worship only Him. He proclaims to them that God is the Creator of heaven and earth, the sea, and the springs of water. The mes-sage for today's world is no different.

Accept Christ as Lord and Savior now, or face Him as Judge later. The good news of the gospel is for every nation and tribe and language and people. Are your ears on?

And they sing the song of Moses, the servant of
God, and the song of the Lamb. (Rev. 15:3)

John saw in heaven those believers, who were redeemed during the tribulation, gathered around the throne of God. They were able to overcome because of their unwavering faith in the Lord Jesus Christ. They are seen holding harps of God, which suggests that they are rejoicing and singing praises to God. It's interesting to note that in the Bible, all of the songs written and sung by God's people make mention of His name or names. The biblical songwriters did not refer to God with pronouns only. Many of the modern contemporary gospel or inspirational songs don't even mention God's name. Gospel artists sometimes agree with record producers and producers of television shows to use pronouns only in their recordings and performances. Rather than lifting up the names of the Father and Son, they compromise for the sake of crossover appeal and a payday. In the song of Moses, God's name is mentioned some thirteen times, and there are pronouns that refer to God some thirty-five times. Like the song of Moses, the song of the Lamb expresses themes of God's faithfulness, deliverance of His people, and judgment of His enemies. A phrase in the song says, "Who will not fear, O Lord, and glorify Your name" (Rev. 15:4)? We can't glorify His name if we're ashamed of saying His name. In our singing, we ought to say His name! Say and sing His name!

They cursed the name of God who had power over these plagues. They did not repent and give Him glory. People gnawed their tongues in anguish and cursed the God of heaven for their pain and sores. They did not repent of their deeds. (Rev. 16:9–11)

Because mankind is so desperately depraved, it is within the unredeemed human to curse God, even while covered in harmful and painful sores. When the sea has become like the blood of a corpse, and every living creature who lives and swims in the sea has died, unsaved mankind will still curse the God of heaven. When the sun begins to scorch people with fierce heat, those who are antichrist will continue to follow the Antichrist, and curse the name of God. When the kingdom of darkness is plunged into an even deeper and darker darkness, those who have rejected Christ will gnaw their tongues in anguish because of the excruciating pain, and with gnawed tongues they will curse the God of heaven who made man's mouth. The apostle John also notes that after cursing the name of God, they did not repent and give Him glory. After cursing the God of heaven, they did not repent of their deeds. We sometimes ask the question, "What will it take for God to get their attention?" The truth is, God is always trying to tell all of us something. He speaks to us through plagues and pandemics. He pursues even as He punishes. But His voice will often go unheard and unheeded. We also ask, "How can this be?" The prophet Jeremiah has an answer. He says, "The heart is deceitful above all things, and desperately wicked; who can know it" (Jer. 17:9)? Lord, You know.

They will make war on the Lamb, and the Lamb will conquer them, for He is Lord of lords and King of kings, and those with Him are called and chosen and faithful. (Rev. 17:14)

When the church was in the days of its infancy, the high priest and the party of the Sadducees arrested the apostles and put them in prison. This was done because of jealousy. But during the night, an angel of the Lord opened the prison doors and brought them out, and said, "Go and stand in the temple and speak to the people all the words of this Life" (Acts 5:20). The apostles immediately obeyed. Afterward they were brought before the Sanhedrin Council where they were questioned and reminded that they had been strictly forbidden to teach in the name of Jesus. But Peter and the apostles answered, "We must obey God rather than men" (Acts 5:29). The members of the council were enraged and wanted to kill them. But Gamaliel, a Pharisee and well respected teacher of the law, spoke. He said, "Keep away from these men and let them alone, for if this plan or undertaking is of man, it will fail; but if it is of God, you will not be able to overthrow them. You might even be found opposing God" (Acts 5:38-39). The plan of Satan and the Antichrist will be to wage war against the Lamb. Those who they have deceived will blindly follow them into battle only to be slaughtered by the Lamb. God's side is always the winning side. Those who are with Him are called, chosen and faithful. Their names are written in the Lamb's book of life. He is Lord of lords and King of kings.

Come out of her, my people, lest you take part
in her sins, lest you share in her plagues; for her
sins are heaped high as heaven, and God has
remembered her iniquities. (Rev. 18:4–5)

In chapter 18 of the book of Revelation, Babylon represents the kingdom of the beast who is the Antichrist. The church, the bride of the Lamb, is the dwelling place of God; Babylon, on the other hand, is the dwelling place of Satan. The voice came from heaven, calling for God's people to come out of Babylon so that they would not participate in her sin and so that they would not receive the plagues of God's wrath that would befall her. This admonition is similar to ones given by the prophet Jeremiah.

Jeremiah said, "Flee from the midst of Babylon; let everyone save his life! Be not cut off in her punishment, for this is the time of the Lord's vengeance, the repayment he is rendering her" (Jer. 51:6). In every age, God's chosen people have had to remove themselves from all that is worldly and ungodly. Today it seems as though many who bear the name "Christian" are becoming more and more like the world, taking part in its blatant sinfulness. God's remembering Babylon's iniquities reveals that He has not turned a blind eye to her wickedness, but is heaping up judgment just as her sins are heaped high as heaven. For those who are in the world but not of it, He says, "For I will be merciful toward their iniquities, and I will remember their sins no more" (Heb. 8:12).

Blessed are those who are invited to the marriage supper of the Lamb. (Rev. 19:9)

The book of Revelation begins and ends with promises of blessing to those who read and obey it. In total, the book contains seven promises of blessing, or beatitudes. A beatitude is a declaration of blessedness. Those who are called/invited to the marriage supper of the Lamb are indeed blessed. Who are those who have been called/invited to the marriage supper of the Lamb? They are of every nation, people, and tongue, who have believed in the gospel of Jesus Christ for salvation. They have washed their robes and made them white in the blood of the Lamb. Truly blessed beyond the description of words are those who have been called by God's sovereign grace to join the Lamb and to worship in His presence throughout all eternity.

And he seized the dragon, that ancient serpent,
who is the devil and Satan, and bound him for
a thousand years, and threw him into the pit,
and shut it and sealed it over him, so that he
might not deceive the nations any longer, until
the thousand years were ended. And the devil
who had deceived them was thrown into the
lake of fire and sulfur where the beast and the
false prophet were, and they will be tormented
day and night forever and ever. (Rev. 20:2, 10)

This is the only place in Scripture where Satan is bound, and the one who is given authority to bind him is the angel who comes down from heaven holding the key to the bottomless pit and a great chain. Not only is he bound in the bottomless pit for a thousand years, but he is bound for (on his way to) the lake of fire and sulfur to be tormented day and night throughout eternity.

Some of us need to understand that we cannot bind Satan; God hasn't given us that authority. On the two occasions that Jesus spoke of "binding and loosing," He was referring to the local church's authority to forgive or discipline wayward members according to the Word of God. (Matt. 16:19; 18:18)

Surely Satan will be bound prior to the inauguration of "the millennium," the thousand-year reign of Christ on earth. After this he will be released for a moment, only to be banished to the lake of fire and sulfur to be tormented forever. Lord, Your kingdom come; Your will be done. Amen.

> *He will wipe away every tear from their eyes,*
> *and death shall be no more, neither shall there*
> *be mourning nor crying nor pain anymore, for*
> *the former things have passed away. (Rev. 21:4)*

Jesus spoke of "weeping and gnashing of teeth" seven times. This expression describes the unending miseries and agonies of hell. Those who spend eternity there will experience inconsolable grief and excruciating pain and anguish. But for those who have been washed in the blood of the Lamb, eternity will be quite different. God's dwelling will be with humanity, and He will live with them. They will be His people, and God Himself will be with them and will be their God. (Rev. 21:3) The redeemed will experience an intimacy with God unlike anything previously known. In heaven, there will be nothing that causes one to be sorrowful. For the redeemed, this will be the end of tears; God will wipe them all away. In heaven, there will be no death, mourning, crying, or pain. All of the effects of the fall will be no more. The redeemed will live in glorified bodies as they enjoy indescribable bliss in the presence of God and the Lamb. In Psalm 16:11, David said, "You make known to me the path of life; in Your presence there is fullness of joy; at Your right hand are pleasures forevermore." When we see Jesus; amen!

And the Spirit and the Bride say, "Come." And let the one who hears say, "Come." And let the one who is thirsty come; let the one who desires take the water of life without price. (Rev. 22:17)

Revelation 22:17 is the final invitation to discipleship that's extended in the Holy Bible. It is the last appeal made to sinners to trust Christ for eternal salvation. The prophet Isaiah extended an invitation in 55:1, saying, "Come, everyone who thirsts, come to the waters; and he who has no money, come, buy and eat! Come, buy wine and milk without money and without price." Jesus extended an invitation in Matthew 11:28–30, saying, "Come to Me, all who labor and are heavy laden, and I will give you rest. Take My yoke upon you, and learn from Me, for I am gentle and lowly in heart, and you will find rest for your souls. For My yoke is easy, and My burden is light." In this final invitation, the Holy Spirit says, "Come." The bride of the Lamb, who is the church, says, "Come." All of the redeemed who have heard and believed the gospel message say, "Come." The one who is spiritually thirsty is invited to come and partake of the living water that Christ offers. Everyone who desires is invited to take the water of life freely without price. Jesus said to the Samaritan woman at Jacob's well, "Whoever drinks of the water that I shall give him will never thirst. But the water that I shall give him will become in him a fountain of water springing up into everlasting life" (John 4:14). The invitation is extended, and the door of the church is open.

CPSIA information can be obtained
at www.ICGtesting.com
Printed in the USA
BVHW080003190922
647356BV00001B/42